German Phrase Book

German translation by
Ellen Dix

German
Phrase Book

Edmund Swinglehurst

NEWNES·BOOKS

NEWNES·BOOKS

First published in 1979 by
The Hamlyn Publishing Group Limited
Published in 1983 by Newnes Books,
84–88, The Centre, Feltham, Middlesex, England

© Copyright The Hamlyn Publishing Group Limited 1979
and Newnes Books, a division of
the Hamlyn Publishing Group Limited 1983

Eighth Impression 1985

ISBN 0 600 34052 X

Printed in Great Britain by
Hazell Watson & Viney Limited,
Member of the BPCC Group,
Aylesbury, Bucks

Distributed in the U.S. by
Larousse & Co. Inc., 572 Fifth Avenue, New York,
New York 10036.

Contents

Introduction

The Newnes German Phrase Book is designed to help the
reader who has no previous knowledge of the language. With
its aid he should be able to make himself readily understood
on all occasions and to cope with the host of minor problems –
and some major ones – that can arise when on holiday or
travelling in Germany.

The key to successful speech in a foreign language is
pronunciation, and an outline of the principles of vowel and
consonant sounds and their usage in German is to be found at
the beginning of this book. This is followed by a section
dealing with the essential elements of German grammar. A
close study of these two sections and constant reference to
them will be of the utmost value: with the pattern of sentence
construction in mind and a feeling for the sound of the
language, the reader will be well equipped to use the phrases
in this book.

These are set out in logical order, beginning with the
various means of travel and entry to the country. The section
on accommodation covers the whole range from hotels and
private houses and villas to youth hostels and camping sites.
Particular attention is paid in the chapter on eating and
drinking to the many varieties of German sausage and the
selection of famous Rhine wines. Shopping, too, is covered in
detail: whether the reader wishes to buy a lens for his
German camera or to equip his self-catering apartment with a
week's supply of groceries, he will find a choice of phrases
easy to refer to and simple to use.

Entertainment, sightseeing, public services, and general
conversations in the hotel bar are all covered, and there is an
important section of commercial and banking phrases of

particular value to the businessman. In addition to carefully chosen phrases, each section includes an appropriate vocabulary which is as comprehensive as possible, and at the end of the book there are quick-reference metric conversion tables for the more important temperatures, weights and measures.

The Newnes German Phrase Book will not only enable the traveller to handle any situation with confidence but will help to make his stay in Germany a more enjoyable one.

Guide to German Pronunciation

This is intended for people with no previous knowledge of German and is based on English pronunciation. This means that it is not entirely accurate but the reader who pays careful attention to this section should, with practice, be able to make himself understood reasonably well in German.

The Vowels

LETTER	APPROXIMATE PRONUNCIATION	EXAMPLE
a	1 short, like *u* in but	**lassen**
	2 long, like *a* in father	**Wagen**
ä	1 short, like *e* in bed	**Bäcker**
	2 long, like *a* in mate	**spät**
e	1 short, like *e* in bed	**Bett**
	2 long, like *a* in mate	**gehen**
	3 in unstressed syllables like *er* in sister	**bringen**
i	1 short, like *i* in bit	**mit**
	2 long, like *ee* in feed	**dir**
ie	like *ee* in feed	**viel**
o	1 short, as *o* in not	**Gott**
	2 long, as *o* in vote	**so**
ō	like *ur* in curtain	**schön**
u	1 short, like *oo* in foot	**rund**
	2 long, like *oo* in food	**Schuh**

Pronunciation

ü	no exact English equivalent; round the lips to say *oo* and try to say *ee*. Close to sound of *ew* in few.	**Hüte, Schüler**
y	like *ü*	**Symbol**

Vowel Sounds Written as Two Letters

ei (occasionally ai, ay and ey)	like *ie* in tie	**dein**
au	like *ow* in vow	**faul**
eu, äu	like *oy* in toy	**neu, äusser**

Note that in German vowels are generally short when followed by two or more consonants and long when followed by the same vowel, by h or by one consonant.

The Consonants

LETTER	APPROXIMATE PRONUNCIATION	EXAMPLE
c, f, h, k, l, m, n, p, t, x	pronounced as in English	
b	1 at the end of a word or syllable like *p* in tap	**ab**
	2 elsewhere as in English	**Bier**
ch	like *ch* in Scottish loch	**ich, doch**
d	1 at the end of a word or syllable like *t* in tip	**Bad**
	2 elsewhere as in English	**denken**
g	1 usually like *g* in go	**gehen**
	2 like *ch* in loch in the ending *-ig*	**billig**

2

j	like *y* in yet	**Jahr**
kn	in words beginning *kn* both sounds are pronounced	**Knopf**
qu	pronounced as two separate sounds: *k* followed by *v*	**Quittung**
r	a slightly rolled sound	**rein**
s	1 before a vowel like *z* in zoo	**sein**
	2 before *p* or *t* like *sh* in ship	**Speise, stimmen**
	3 elsewhere like *s* in set	**das**
sch	like *sh* in ship	**Schaf**
ss	like *s* in set	**besser**
th	like *t* in top	**Theater**
tsch	like *ch* in church	**deutsch**
tz	like *ts* in cats	**Platz**
v	like *f* in fat	**vor**
w	like *v* in vase	**Wasser**
z	like *ts* in cats	**Zimmer**

A Little Grammar in Action

Nouns and adjectives

All nouns in German belong to one of three genders, that is, they are either masculine, feminine or neuter, irrespective of whether they refer to living beings or inanimate objects. The word for 'the' or definite article, **der**, changes according to the gender of the noun it precedes. Nouns in German are spelt with a capital letter.

MASCULINE **der Mann** the man
FEMININE **die Frau** the woman
NEUTER **das Kind** the child

There are four cases in German: nominative or subject case; accusative or object case; genitive or possessive case; and dative or indirect object case. The ending of the noun declines, that is, it changes according to which case it is in. Similarly, the word for 'the' also varies, and any adjective accompanying the noun likewise changes its endings. There is no room here to deal with the declensions of the various categories into which German nouns are divided, nor with the different ways in which German nouns form their plurals. Instead, we have chosen examples of common declensions.

	SINGULAR		PLURAL
MASCULINE			
Nominative	**der junge Mann**	the young man	**die jungen Männer**
Accusative	**den jungen Mann**	the young man	**die jungen Männer**
Genitive	**des jungen Mannes**	of the young man	**der jungen Männer**
Dative	**dem jungen Mann**	to the young man	**den jungen Männern**

4

	SINGULAR		PLURAL

FEMININE

Nominative	die alte Frau	the old woman	die alten Frauen
Accusative	die alte Frau	the old woman	die alten Frauen
Genitive	der alten Frau	of the old woman	der alten Frauen
Dative	der alten Frau	to the old woman	den alten Frauen

NEUTER

Nominative	das kleine Kind	the small child	die kleinen Kinder
Accusative	das kleine Kind	the small child	die kleinen Kinder
Genitive	des kleinen Kindes	of the small child	der kleinen Kinder
Dative	dem kleinen Kind	to the small child	den kleinen Kindern

The word for 'a' or indefinite article in German is **ein**:

MASCULINE **ein Mann** a man
FEMININE **eine Frau** a woman
NEUTER **ein Kind** a child

When **ein** is used with an adjective and noun the form of the adjective changes slightly:

MASCULINE

Nominative	ein junger Mann	a young man
Accusative	einen jungen Mann	a young man
Genitive	eines jungen Mannes	of a young man
Dative	einem jungen Mann	to a young man

FEMININE

Nominative	eine alte Frau	an old woman
Accusative	eine alte Frau	an old woman
Genitive	einer alten Frau	of an old woman
Dative	einer alten Frau	to an old woman

NEUTER

Nominative	ein kleines Kind	a small child
Accusative	ein kleines Kind	a small child
Genitive	eines kleinen Kindes	of a small child
Dative	einem kleinen Kind	to a small child

5

Grammar

The following are examples of **der** and **ein** used with adjectives and nouns in the four cases.

1 The accusative or object case:

Wir sehen den jungen Mann und ein kleines Kind.
We see the young man and a small child.

2 The genitive or possessive case:

Die Kleider der alten Frau sind hier.
The clothes of the old woman (the old woman's clothes) are here.

3 The dative or indirect case, which is also used with certain prepositions:

Ich gebe dem kleinen Kind ein Buch.
I give a book to the little child.

Die alten Frauen kommen mit dem jungen Mann.
The old women are coming with the young man.

Demonstrative Adjectives

The words for 'this' and 'that' are **dieser** and **jener** respectively, which are declined in the same way as **der**, **die** and **das**.

	MASCULINE	FEMININE	NEUTER	PLURAL
Nominative	dieser	diese	dieses	diese
Accusative	diesen	diese	dieses	diese
Genitive	dieses	dieser	dieses	dieser
Dative	diesem	dieser	diesem	diesen

Examples are as follows:

Ich lese dieses Buch. I am reading this book.

Jenes Kind ist mein Sohn. That boy is my son.

Das Ende dieser Strasse. The end of this street.

Er gab jenen Kindern einen Apfel. He gave those children an apple.

6

Possessive Adjectives

The words for 'my', 'your', etc., are declined in the same way as **ein,** depending on the gender of the noun they precede.

	MASCULINE	FEMININE	NEUTER	PLURAL
my	mein	meine	mein	meine
your	dein	deine	dein	deine
his	sein	seine	sein	seine
her	ihr	ihre	ihr	ihre
its	sein	seine	sein	seine
our	unser	unsere	unser	unsere
your	euer	euere	euer	euere
your	Ihr	Ihre	Ihr	Ihre
their	ihr	ihre	ihr	ihre

Note that **dein** and its plural **euer** are familiar forms of 'your', used only with members of the family, children, or close friends.

Ihr, always spelt with a capital 'i', is the word to use for 'your' when speaking to all other people.

Examples are as follows:

Ich sehe meinen Onkel. I see my uncle.

Er sprach mit ihrem Vater. He spoke with her father.

Seine Mutter kommt jetzt. His mother is coming now.

Ist das Ihr Buch? Is that your book?

Personal Pronouns

The words for 'I', 'you', 'he', etc., are as follows.

1 When used as the subject of a verb:

Ich singe	I sing
du singst	you sing
er singt	he sings
sie singt	she sings
es singt	it sings
wir singen	we sing
ihr singt	you sing
sie singen	they sing
Sie singen	you sing

2 When used as the direct object of a verb:

Herr Braun sieht mich	Mr Brown sees	me
	dich	you
	ihn	him
	sie	her
	es	it
	uns	us
	euch	you
	sie	them
	Sie	you

3 When used as the indirect object of a verb:

Herr Braun sagt	**mir**	Mr Brown says to me
	dir	to you
	ihm	to him
	ihr	to her
	ihm	to it
	uns	to us
	euch	to you
	ihnen	to them
	Ihnen	to you

Du, its plural **ihr**, and **dich, dir, euch**, etc., are the familiar forms of 'you' and 'to you', and should only be used with members of the family, children or close friends.
Sie, always spelt with a capital *S*, is the word to use when speaking to all other people. Note that **sie**, spelt with a small *s*, means either 'she' or 'her', 'they' or 'them'.

4 When used after a preposition:

In German some prepositions are followed by a noun or pronoun in the accusative or direct object case:

Diese Bücher sind für mich	These books are for me
dich	you
ihn	him
sie	her
es	it
uns	us
euch	you
sie	them
Sie	you

Others are followed by a noun or pronoun in the dative or indirect object case:

Der Mann kommt mit mir	The man is coming with me
dir	you
ihm	him
ihr	her
ihm	it
uns	us
euch	you
ihnen	them
Ihnen	you

Grammar

Prepositions followed by the accusative case include:

durch through
für for
gegen against, towards
ohne without
um round
wider against

Prepositions followed by the dative case include:

aus out
bei by, near
mit with
nach to, after
seit since
von of, from
zu to

Verbs

German verbs are too complicated for detailed discussion in a phrase book, but for the traveller who wants a quick grasp of verbs with which he can communicate while travelling in German-speaking countries, the following basic rules will be useful.

Strong and Irregular Verbs

These are verbs which change their form when conjugated, although not all do so in the present tense, which is shown here. They include some of the most common verbs in German.

sein to be

ich bin I am
du bist you are
er ist he is
sie ist she is
es ist it is
wir sind we are
ihr seid you are
sie sind they are
Sie sind you are

dürfen to be allowed, may

ich darf I may
du darfst you may
er darf he may
sie darf she may
es darf it may
wir dürfen we may
ihr dürft you may
sie dürfen they may
Sie dürfen you may

gehen to go

ich gehe I go
du gehst you go
er geht he goes
sie geht she goes
es geht it goes
wir gehen we go
ihr geht you go
sie gehen they go
Sie gehen you go

können to be able, can

ich kann I can
du kannst you can

haben to have

ich habe I have
du hast you have
er hat he has
sie hat she has
es hat it has
wir haben we have
ihr habt you have
sie haben they have
Sie haben you have

geben to give

ich gebe I give
du gibst you give
er gibt he gives
sie gibt she gives
es gibt it gives
wir geben we give
ihr gebt you give
sie geben they give
Sie geben you give

kommen to come

ich komme I come
du kommst you come
er kommt he comes
sie kommt she comes
es kommt it comes
wir kommen we come
ihr kommt you come
sie kommen they come
Sie kommen you come

mögen to like

ich mag I like
du magst you like

er kann he can
sie kann she can
es kann it can
wir können we can
ihr könnt you can
sie können they can
Sie können you can

müssen to have to, must

ich muss I must
du musst you must
er muss he must
sie muss she must
es muss it must
wir müssen we must
ihr müsst you must
sie müssen she must
Sie müssen you must

sollen ought, should

ich soll I ought
du sollst you ought
er soll he ought
sie soll she ought
es soll it ought
wir sollen we ought
ihr sollt you ought
sie sollen they ought
Sie sollen you ought

werden to become

ich werde I become
du wirst you become
er wird he becomes
sie wird she becomes
es wird it becomes
wir werden we become

er mag he likes
sie mag she likes
es mag it likes
wir mögen we like
ihr mögt you like
sie mögen they like
Sie mögen you like

sehen to see

ich sehe I see
du siehst you see
er sieht he sees
sie sieht she sees
es sieht it sees
wir sehen we see
ihr seht you see
sie sehen they see
Sie sehen you see

sprechen to speak

ich spreche I speak
du sprichst you speak
er spricht he speaks
sie spricht she speaks
es spricht it speaks
wir sprechen we speak
ihr sprecht you speak
sie sprechen they speak
Sie sprechen you speak

wollen to want to, wish

ich will I wish
du willst you wish
er will he wishes
sie will she wishes
es will it wishes
wir wollen we wish

ihr werdet you become
sie werden they become
Sie werden you become

ihr wollt you wish
sie wollen they wish
Sie wollen you wish

Weak Verbs

Many verbs in German, the so-called weak verbs, change only their endings when conjugated:

lachen laugh

ich lache I laugh
du lachst you laugh
er lacht he laughs
sie lacht she laughs
es lacht it laughs
wir lachen we laugh
ihr lacht you laugh
sie lachen they laugh
Sie lachen you laugh

hören to hear

ich höre I hear
du hörst you hear
er hört he hears
sie hört she hears
es hört it hears
wir hören we hear
ihr hört you hear
sie hören they hear
Sie hören you hear

To form the negative of a verb **nicht** is added after it.

Sie lacht nicht. She doesn't laugh.

Ich sehe den Mann nicht. I don't see the man.

In most cases a simple statement can be turned into a question simply by putting the verb before the subject.

Raucht er englische Zigaretten? Does he smoke English cigarettes?

Gehen Sie heute ins Kino? Are you going to the cinema today?

German Spoken

German is spoken in Switzerland and Austria as well as in Germany, and there are many other parts of Europe where it is the second language of the inhabitants.

Germany

Five important German towns lie in regions that are each world famous in their own way.

HAMBURG on the Alster and the biggest town after Berlin has been a leading German seaport since the times of the Hanseatic League. Although its notorious Reeperbahn, with its nightclubs and brothels, has given Hamburg sensational publicity, the city has much besides in the way of old and modern buildings, art galleries and fine boulevards.

COLOGNE is where the southbound traveller discovers why the river Rhine is so renowned. Castles tower on the steep, vineyard-covered sides and there are legends at every turn, including those of Snow White and the Seven Dwarfs and the famous Rhinemaidens. Bonn, Beethoven's birthplace, is up river and Wiesbaden, a spa, and Frankfurt, an important city, lie to the south.

BADEN-BADEN, the most famous spa in Europe, where aristocrats and artists had their romantic escapades and lost money at the gambling tables, is still an attractive holiday town and is the gateway to the Black Forest.

MUNICH, perhaps the most appealing of all German towns, is in Bavaria, a wonderland of mountains and lakes, where Hitler built his Eagle's Nest at Berchtesgaden. The vast beerhalls provide amazing and unique entertainment and there are exuberant rococo buildings and art galleries.

BERLIN, the old capital city of Germany, isolated in its eastern German territory, is now a modern metropolis divided by the Wall. On the western side there is much to do and see and endless entertainment.

Austria

For English-speaking people there are three Austrias. First the Austria of the capital, Vienna, with its cafés and cream cakes, the Spanish Riding School and the Opera. Here Strauss waltzes still seem the appropriate accompaniment to daily life. Then there is the Tyrol, the land of wooden chalets, mountains, pine forests, and peasant dress, whose capital is Innsbruck. And a little farther east lies Salzburg, birthplace of Mozart and a town of Italian-style architecture, near which lie the lakes of Salzkammergut, with St Wolfgang and the White Horse Inn.

To the south lies another Austria, less well known to the English visitor. This is Carinthia, a land of warm lakes and wooded hills and an old-fashioned tempo of living.

Switzerland

The German-speaking part of Switzerland has Zürich as its capital and includes the great mountains of the Bernese Oberland and the Engadine.

Wherever you travel in these countries, you will find a few words spoken in their language will help to establish a friendly atmosphere.

Here to start with are some simple expressions of greetings:

Good morning	**Guten Morgen**
Good afternoon	**Guten Tag**
Good evening	**Guten Abend**
Good night	**Gute Nacht**
How are you?	**Wie geht es Ihnen?**
I'm very pleased to meet you	**Ich freue mich, Sie kennenzulernen**
How do you do?	**Guten Tag**
Goodbye	**Auf Wiedersehen**

Some words of courtesy:

Please	**Bitte**
Thank you	**Danke**
It's very kind of you	**Das ist sehr nett von Ihnen**
You are welcome	**Bitte sehr**
Not at all	**Nichts zu danken**

And some questions:

Where is the hotel?	**Wo ist das Hotel?**
What did you say?	**Was haben Sie gesagt?**
When does the train leave?	**Wann fährt der Zug ab?**
Who are you?	**Wer sind Sie?**
How much does it cost?	**Wieviel kostet es?**
Which is the road to ...?	**Welche Strasse führt nach ...?**
Why are we waiting?	**Warum warten wir?**

Finally some useful common phrases:

Yes.	**Ja, jawohl.**
No.	**Nein.**
Why?	**Warum?**
How?	**Wie?**
When?	**Wann?**
What?	**Was?**
Where?	**Wo?**
How much?	**Wieviel?**
How many?	**Wieviele?**
Please speak slowly.	**Bitte sprechen Sie langsam.**
I do not understand German very well.	**Ich verstehe Deutsch nicht sehr gut.**
Will you write it down please?	**Würden Sie das bitte aufschreiben?**
How do I say?	**Wie sage ich ...?**
What is the meaning of ...?	**Was bedeutet ...?**
Please explain how this works.	**Bitte, erklären Sie, wie dies funktioniert.**
How far is it to ...?	**Wie weit ist es nach ...?**
Where is the nearest ...?	**Wo ist der nächste ...?**
What time is it?	**Wie spät ist es?**
Will you please help me?	**Würden Sie mir bitte helfen?**
Can you point to where we are on this map?	**Können Sie mir bitte auf dieser Karte zeigen, wo wir sind?**

Which way do I go?	**Wie komme ich dahin?**
Is there an official tourist office here?	**Gibt es hier ein Fremdenverkehrsbüro?**
Where is the station/bus terminus/bus stop?	**Wo ist der Bahnhof/die Busendstation/die Bushaltestelle?**
Where do I buy a ticket?	**Wo kauft man die Fahrkarte?**
Am I too early?	**Bin ich zu früh gekommen?**
It is too late.	**Es ist zu spät.**
We have missed the train.	**Wir haben den Zug verpasst.**
Do I turn right/left?	**Biege ich rechts/links ab?**
Do I go straight ahead?	**Gehe ich geradeaus?**
What is the name of this street?	**Wie heisst diese Strasse?**
How do I get to ...?	**Wie komme ich nach ...?**
It is too expensive.	**Es ist zu teuer.**
Please give me the change.	**Ich bekomme Geld zurück.**
I am tired/hungry/thirsty.	**Ich bin müde/hungrig/durstig.**
It is very hot/cold.	**Es ist sehr heiss/kalt.**
Please take me to my hotel.	**Bitte, bringen Sie mich zu meinem Hotel.**
Is the service included?	**Ist Bedienung einbegriffen?**
Thank you very much.	**Vielen Dank.**

And some idiomatic expressions

Go away.	**Gehen Sie weg!**

Leave me alone.	**Lassen Sie mich in Ruhe.**
Shut up.	**Halten Sie den Mund.**
Oh Hell!	**Mein Gott!**
How goes it?	**Wie geht's?**
So so.	**Einigermassen.**
You're joking.	**Das kann doch nicht wahr sein.**
Don't move.	**Rühren Sie sich nicht, bitte.**
That's it.	**So ist das.**
You're right.	**Sie haben recht.**
Carry on.	**Weiter, bitte.**

All Aboard

Journeys through German-speaking Europe are made easy by the excellent means of communication and interesting because of the centuries of history that have left their mark on every town and village. In Germany you can get about easily on internal air services, but travel by rail or road is more rewarding. Railways are fast and go through some magnificent scenery, especially in the Rhine valley, the Black Forest and Bavaria. In Austria much of the scenery is alpine.

The types of train in operation are:

TEE	A high-speed Trans-Europe Express.
Fernschnellzug	A long-distance train stopping only at the principal stations. In Austria and Switzerland this is called an Express.
D-Zug	An Express but with more stops. Called **Schnellzug** in Austria and Switzerland.
Personenzug	A local train.
Triebwagen	These are diesel-driven coaches for local services.

Germany's autobahns and roads are excellent and there are plenty of service stations and refreshment areas. In the south there are picturesque but slower routes that wind through beautiful scenery. The Romantic Road between the River Main and the Bavarian Alps is one such route; another is the Bavarian Alpine road. Yet another way to enjoy travelling in Germany is by boat. On the Rhine there are several steamer companies which travel from Strasbourg to the mouth of the river.

Arrivals and Departures

Going through Passport Control and Customs

At most of the main gateway airports and ports there will be
someone with a smattering of English, but this is not the case
at all frontier posts. It is useful, therefore, to know one or two
basic phrases. Apart from making communication easier, they
help to establish a friendly relationship with officials and
often smooth the passage through frontiers.

Good morning/afternoon/ evening.	**Guten Morgen/guten Tag/ guten Abend.**
Here is my passport/visitor's card.	**Hier is mein Reisepass/ meine Besucherkarte.**
I am on holiday/on business.	**Ich bin auf Urlaub hier/auf Geschäftsreise.**
I am visiting relatives/friends.	**Ich besuche Verwandte/ Freunde.**
Here is my vaccination certificate.	**Hier ist mein Impfschein.**
The visa is stamped on page ...	**Das Visum ist auf Seite ... gestempelt.**
They did not stamp my passport at the entry port.	**Man hat meinen Pass am Einreisehafen nicht gestempelt.**
Will you please stamp my passport? It will be a souvenir of my holiday.	**Würden Sie bitte meinen Pass stempeln? Als Andenken an meinen Urlaub.**
I will be staying a few days/two weeks/a month.	**Ich bleibe ein paar Tage/zwei Wochen/einen Monat.**
I am just passing through.	**Ich bin auf der Durchreise.**

21

My wife and I have a joint passport.	**Meine Frau und ich haben einen gemeinsamen Pass.**
The children are on my wife's passport.	**Die Personalien der Kinder stehen im Pass meiner Frau.**
I didn't realise it had expired.	**Ich hatte nicht gewusst, dass er abgelaufen war.**
Can I telephone the British consulate?	**Darf ich bitte das Britische Konsulat anrufen?**
I have nothing to declare.	**Ich habe nichts zu verzollen.**
Do you want me to open my cases? Which one?	**Soll ich meine Koffer öffnen? Welchen?**
They are all personal belongings.	**Das sind alles meine persönlichen Sachen.**
I have a few small gifts for my friends.	**Ich habe ein paar kleine Geschenke für meine Freunde.**
I have 200 cigarettes, some wine and a bottle of spirits.	**Ich habe zweihundert Zigaretten, etwas Wein und eine Flasche Schnaps.**
They are for my personal consumption.	**Das ist für meinen persönlichen Verbrauch.**
Do I have to pay duty?	**Muss ich Zoll bezahlen?**
I have no other luggage.	**Ich habe weiter kein Gepäck.**
Do you want to see my handbag/briefcase?	**Soll ich meine Handtasche/Aktenmappe aufmachen?**
I can't find my keys.	**Ich kann meine Schlüssel nicht finden.**
I have 200 Deutschmarks in currency, 100 Deutschmarks in travellers' cheques.	**Ich habe zweihundert Deutschmark in Bargeld, hundert in Reiseschecks.**

I can't afford to pay duty.	**Ich kann den Zoll nicht bezahlen.**
Can you keep it in bond?	**Können Sie es unter Zollverschluss legen?**
Here is a list of the souvenirs I have bought.	**Hier ist eine Liste der Andenken, die ich gekauft habe.**
You haven't marked my suitcase.	**Sie haben meinen Koffer nicht markiert.**
May I leave now?	**Kann ich jetzt gehen?**

At Airports, Terminals and Stations

Where can I find a porter?	**Wo kann ich einen Gepäckträger bekommen?**
Where can I find a luggage trolley?	**Wo gibt es Gepäckwagen?**
Where can I find the left luggage office?	**Wo ist die Gepäckaufbewahrung?**
Where can I find my registered luggage?	**Wo bekomme ich mein Gepäck, das ich aufgegeben habe?**
Have you seen the representative of my travel company?	**Wissen Sie, wo der Vertreter meiner Reisegesellschaft ist?**
Please take my bag to the bus/taxi/car.	**Bitte, bringen Sie meinen Koffer zum Bus/Taxi/Auto.**
How much per case?	**Wie teuer ist es pro Koffer?**

Toilets

Is there a ladies' toilet/gentlemen's toilet?	**Gibt es hier eine Damentoilette/eine Herrentoilette?**

Have you any soap?
  toilet paper?
  a clean towel?
  a comb or hairbrush?
	**Haben Sie Seife?
	  Toilettenpapier?
	  ein sauberes Handtuch?
	  einen Kamm oder eine Haarbürste?**

Shall I leave a tip?	**Muss man Trinkgeld geben?**

Telephone

Where are the public telephones?	**Wo sind die Telefonzellen?**
I need a telephone directory.	**Ich brauche ein Telefonbuch.**
Where can I get some change?	**Wo kann ich Kleingeld bekommen?**
Can I dial this number or do I ask the operator?	**Kann ich diese Nummer selbst wählen oder geht es durchs Amt?**
Hullo.	**Hallo.**
May I have Bonn 12345?	**Können Sie mich mit Bonn eins dreiundzwanzigfünfundvierzig verbinden?**
Can I reverse the charges?	**Ich möchte ein R-Gespräch bitte.**
I want a person-to-person call.	**Ich möchte ein Gespräch mit Voranmeldung.**
I have been cut off.	**Wir sind unterbrochen worden.**
You gave me the wrong number.	**Ich bin falsch verbunden worden.**
Is she not in?	**Ist sie nicht da?**
Tell her I called. My name is ...	**Sagen Sie ihr bitte, dass ich angerufen habe. Mein Name ist ...**

Signs

Booking Office	**Fahrkartenschalter**
Cars Check-in Desk	**Anmeldeschalter-Autos**

Coach Station	**Reisebus-Bahnhof**
Exit	**Ausgang**
Escalator	**Rolltreppe**
Information Office	**Auskunftsbüro**
Left Luggage	**Gepäckaufbewahrung**
Porters	**Gepäckträger**
Toilet	**Toilette**
Platform	**Bahnsteig**
Underground	**U-Bahn**
Waiting Room	**Wartesaal**

Taxi Rank

Where can I get a taxi?	**Wo kann ich ein Taxi bekommen?**
Please get me a taxi.	**Besorgen Sie mir bitte ein Taxi.**
Take me to Kaiserstrasse 25.	**Fahren Sie mich bitte zur Kaiserstrasse fünfundzwanzig.**
How much will it cost?	**Was kostet das?**
That's too much.	**Das ist zu teuer.**
Turn right/left. Turn at the next corner.	**Rechts/links abbiegen. An der nächsten Ecke abbiegen.**
Go straight on.	**Geradeaus.**
I'll tell you when to stop.	**Ich sage Ihnen, wo Sie halten müssen.**
Stop.	**Halt.**

I'm in a hurry.	**Ich habe es eilig.**
Take it easy.	**Langsam, bitte.**
Can you please carry my bags?	**Würden Sie bitte mein Gepäck tragen?**

Newsstand/Kiosk

Have you got English papers or magazines?	**Haben Sie englische Zeitungen oder Illustrierte?**
Have you any paperbacks?	**Haben Sie Taschenbücher?**
Is there a local paper?	**Gibt es eine Lokalzeitung?**
Do you sell timetables?	**Verkaufen Sie Fahrpläne?**
Have you a guide/map to the city?	**Haben Sie einen Stadtführer/ Stadtplan?**
Have you any writing paper and envelopes?	**Haben Sie Schreibpapier und Umschläge?**
sellotape?	**Tesafilm?**
matches?	**Streichhölzer?**
cigarettes?	**Zigaretten?**
stamps?	**Briefmarken?**
a ball-point pen?	**einen Kugelschreiber?**
some string?	**Bindfaden?**

Information Bureau

Is there an information bureau here?	**Gibt es hier ein Auskunftsbüro?**
Have you any leaflets?	**Haben Sie Prospekte?**
Have you a guide to hotels?	**Haben Sie einen Hotelführer?**
pensions?	**ein Verzeichnis von Pensionen?**

27

youth hostels?	**Jugendherbergen?**
camp sites?	**Campingplätzen?**

Do you find accommodation for visitors?	**Vermitteln Sie Unterkunft für Touristen?**
I want a first-class hotel.	**Ich möchte ein erstklassiges Hotel.**
a second-class hotel.	**ein gutes Hotel.**
a pension.	**eine Pension.**
a single room.	**ein Einzelzimmer.**
a double room.	**ein Doppelzimmer.**
We'll go right away.	**Wir möchten sofort hin.**
How do I get there?	**Wie komme ich dahin?**

At Airports

Where is the check-in desk?	**Wo ist der Anmelde-Schalter?**
Can I take this in the cabin?	**Kann ich dies bei mir haben?**
Do I have to pay excess?	**Muss ich Übergewicht bezahlen?**
You haven't given me a luggage claim tag.	**Sie haben mir keinen Gepäckschein gegeben.**
I've missed my flight. Can you give me another flight?	**Ich habe meinen Flug verpasst. Kann ich einen anderen Flug bekommen?**
Is there a bar on the other side of the customs barrier?	**Gibt es eine Bar hinter der Zollbarriere?**
Where is the flight indicator?	**Wo ist der Flugindikator?**
Is there a duty-free shop?	**Gibt es einen zollfreien Laden?**

Is there another way to go up/ down other than by escalator?

Gibt es auch einen Fahrstuhl oder eine Treppe nach oben/ unten?

Where can I get some flight insurance?

Wo kann ich eine Flugversicherung abschliessen?

Is there a wheelchair available?

Kann ich einen Rollstuhl bekommen?

At Railway Stations

Where is the ticket office?

Wo ist der Fahrkartenschalter?

One first-class/second-class return ticket to Munich.

Einmal erster/zweiter Klasse nach München, hin und zurück.

How much is a child's fare?

Wie hoch ist der Kinderfahrpreis?

Can I reserve a seat/a couchette/ a sleeping berth?

Kann ich einen Platz/eine Liege/eine Schlafkoje buchen?

Is there a supplement to pay?

Muss ich Zuschlag zahlen?

Do I have to change?

Muss ich umsteigen?

Will there be a restaurant car/ buffet car on the train?

Gibt es einen Speisewagen/ einen Erfrischungswagen in dem Zug?

Where is the platform for the train to Stuttgart?

Von welchem Gleis fährt der Zug nach Stuttgart?

Does my friend need a platform ticket?

Braucht mein Freund eine Bahnsteigkarte?

At what time does the train leave?

Wann fährt der Zug ab?

Airports, Terminals and Stations

At a Port

Which is quay number six?	**Wo ist Kai Nummer sechs?**
Where is the car ferry terminal?	**Von wo fährt die Autofähre ab?**
At what time can I go on board?	**Wann darf ich an Bord gehen?**
Will there be an announcement when visitors must disembark?	**Wird bekantgegeben, wann Nichtreisende an Land gehen müssen?**

Vocabulary

bench	**die Bank**
bus driver	**der Fahrer**
clock	**die Uhr**
gate	**die Sperre**
guard	**der Schaffner**
left luggage office	**die Gepäckaufbewahrung**
lockers	**die Schliessfächer**
porter	**der Gepäckträger**
security officer	**der Sicherheitsbeamte**
station buffet	**der Erfrischungsraum**
station master	**der Bahnhofsvorsteher**
tannoy	**der Lautsprecher**
ticket collector	**der Schaffner**
vending machine	**der Warenautomat**
waiting room	**der Wartesaal**

En Route

General Expressions

At what time do we start/take off?	**Wann fahren wir ab/starten wir?**
Why is there a delay?	**Warum haben wir Verzögerung?**
Have I got time to go to the toilet?	**Habe ich genug Zeit, zur Toilette zu gehen?**
I have mislaid my ticket.	**Ich habe meine Fahrkarte verlegt.**
Take my address and passport number.	**Bitte notieren Sie meine Adresse und Passnummer.**
Is this seat reserved?	**Ist dieser Sitzplatz reserviert?**

Travelling by Air

Are you the Chief Steward/Stewardess?	**Sind Sie der Chefsteward/die Chefstewardess?**
Which button do I press to call you?	**Welchen Knopf muss ich drücken, wenn ich Sie brauche?**
Can you help me to adjust my seat?	**Können Sie mir bitte mit meinem Sitz helfen?**
Shall I fasten my seat belt?	**Muss ich mich festschnallen?**
I haven't got a sick bag.	**Ich habe keine Spucktüte.**
How high are we flying?	**Wie hoch fliegen wir?**
What speed are we doing?	**Welche Geschwindigkeit haben wir?**

31

Travelling

What town is that down below?	**Wie heisst die Stadt da unten?**
Is there a map of the route?	**Gibt es eine Karte von dieser Strecke?**
Are there any duty-free goods available?	**Kann man hier zollfreie Waren kaufen?**
Can I pay you in foreign currency/English money?	**Kann ich mit ausländischem Geld/mit englischem Geld bezahlen?**
The airvent is stuck.	**Der Ventilator funktioniert nicht.**
May I change my seat?	**Könnte ich meinen Sitzplatz wechseln?**

VOCABULARY

aircraft	**das Flugzeug**
air terminal	**das Flugterminal**
arrival gate	**das Ankunfts-Gate**
ashtray	**der Aschenbecher**
flight deck	**das Flugdeck**
fuselage	**der Flugzeugrumpf**
jet engine	**der Düsenmotor**
light	**das Licht**
luggage shelf	**das Gepäckfach**
propeller	**der Propeller**
tail	**das Schwanzende**
tray meal	**die Tablettmahlzeit**
window	**das Fenster**
wing	**die Tragfläche**

Signs

Fasten your seat belt	**Bitte, festschnallen**
Emergency exit	**Notausgang**
No smoking	**Rauchen verboten**

Travelling by Motor Rail

I have booked my car by rail to Hamburg.	**Ich habe eine Reservierung für meinen Wagen in dem Autoreisezug nach Hamburg.**
Does the ticket include insurance?	**Ist die Fahrkarte einschliesslich Versicherung?**
At what time must I report?	**Wann muss ich mich melden?**
Where is the loading platform?	**Wo ist die Laderampe?**
Shall I lock the car?	**Muss ich das Auto abschliessen?**
Can I leave my belongings in the car?	**Kann ich meine Sachen im Auto lassen?**
Where is our compartment?	**Wo ist unser Abteil?**
At what time do I have to drive off?	**Wann muss ich den Wagen abfahren?**

Travelling by Rail

Can you tell me where carriage 5 is?	**Können Sie mir bitte sagen, wo Wagen fünf ist?**
I have a couchette reservation.	**Ich habe eine Liegewagenreservierung.**
This is my seat reservation.	**Dies ist meine Platzkarte.**

33

Travelling

Is this seat taken?	**Ist dieser Platz besetzt?**
Is the dining car at the front or the back?	**Ist der Speisewagen vorn oder hinten im Zug?**
Two tickets for the first/second service please.	**Zwei Karten für das erste/ zweite Essen bitte.**
Is the buffet car open throughout the journey?	**Ist der Erfrischungswagen während der ganzen Fahrt geöffnet?**
Can I leave my big case in the baggage car?	**Kann ich meinen grossen Koffer im Gepäckwagen lassen?**
Is there an observation car?	**Gibt es einen Aussichtswagen?**
What station is this?	**Welche Station ist dies?**
The heating is on/off/too high/ too low.	**Die Heizung ist an/aus/zu stark/zu schwach.**
I can't open/close the window.	**Ich kann das Fenster nicht öffnen/schliessen.**
Where do I have to change?	**Wo muss ich umsteigen?**
Is this where I get my connection for Mannheim?	**Bekomme ich hier Anschluss nach Mannheim?**

Vocabulary

blanket	**die Decke**
corridor	**der Korridor**
compartment	**das Abteil**
cushion	**das Kissen**
luggage rack	**das Gepäcknetz**
non smoking	**Nichtraucher**
sleeping berth	**die Liege**

34

| sleeping car | der Schlafwagen |
| sliding door | die Schiebetür |

SIGNS

| Do not lean out of the window. | Nicht aus dem Fenster lehnen. |
| Do not use the toilet while the train is standing at the station. | Bitte, nicht den Abort benutzen während der Zug im Bahnhof hält. |

Travelling on a Steamer

Where is the purser's office?	Wo ist das Purser-Büro?
Can you show me my cabin?	Können Sie mir meine Kabine zeigen?
Are you the steward?	Sind Sie der Steward?
Is there a children's nursery/a shop/a gymnasium?	Gibt es ein Kinderzimmer/ein Geschäft/eine Gymnastikhalle?
Where can I get some seasick tablets?	Wo bekomme ich Tabletten gegen Seekrankheit?
On which side do we disembark?	Auf welcher Seite gehen wir an Land?
The sea is calm/rough.	Die See ist ruhig/stürmisch.
What are those birds? Seagulls?	Was für Vögel sind das? Möwen?
Is there a duty-free shop?	Gibt es ein duty-free Shop?

Travelling

aft	**hinten**
anchor	**der Anker**
bridge	**die Brücke**
captain	**der Kapitän**
crew	**die Mannschaft**
danger – propellers	**Vorsicht – Propeller**
deck	**das Deck**
funnel	**der Schornstein**
lifebelt	**der Rettungsring**
lifeboat	**das Rettungsboot**
mast	**der Mast**
officer	**der Offizier**
port (harbour)	**der Hafen**
port (left)	**Das Backbord**
radar	**das Radargerät**
raft	**das Floss**
rail	**die Reling**
starboard	**das Steuerbord**

Travelling by Coach

Is this the coach for Garmisch-Partenkirchen?	**Ist dies der Reisebus nach Garmisch-Partenkirchen?**
Can I sit next to the driver?	**Kann ich beim Fahrer sitzen?**
Are the seats numbered?	**Sind die Plätze numeriert?**
Do I pay on the coach?	**Muss ich im Bus bezahlen?**
Is there a stop en route?	**Wird unterwegs Station gemacht?**
Would you mind closing the window? It's draughty.	**Würden Sie bitte das Fenster schliessen? Es zieht.**

36

Can you help me with my luggage?	**Können Sie mir mit meinem Gepäck helfen?**

VOCABULARY

back seat	**der Rücksitz**
driver	**der Fahrer**
foot rest	**die Fusstütze**
front seat	**der Vordersitz**
guide	**der Reiseführer**
luggage compartment	**der Kofferraum**

Bus and Underground

Where is the bus stop?	**Wo ist die Bushaltestelle?**
Does one have to queue?	**Muss man sich anstellen?**
Can I buy a book of tickets?	**Kann ich ein Fahrscheinheft kaufen?**
Do you go by the Hofgarten?	**Fahren Sie am Hofgarten vorbei?**
Will you tell me when we reach the Hohestrasse?	**Würden Sie mir bitte Bescheid sagen, wenn wir in der Hohestrasse sind?**
I want to get off at the next stop.	**Ich möchte an der nächsten Haltestelle aussteigen.**
Will you ring the bell please?	**Würden Sie bitte auf den Knopf drücken?**
I want to go to the Prater.	**Ich möchte zum Prater.**
Which line do I take?	**Mit welcher Linie muss ich fahren?**

Travelling

Do I have to change?	**Muss ich umsteigen?**
At what time is the last underground train?	**Wann fährt die letzte U-Bahn?**
Here is the metro map. Press the button and your line lights up.	**Hier ist der U-Bahn-Plan. Drücken Sie den Knopf und Ihre Linie leuchtet auf.**

VOCABULARY

automatic door	**die automatische Tür**
barrier	**die Sperre**
escalator	**die Rolltreppe**

SIGNS

Reserved for war wounded	**Für Kriegsbeschädigte reserviert**
Reserved for disabled persons	**Für Körperbehinderte reserviert**

Other Vehicles

Where can I hire a bicycle/a moped/a tricycle/a tandem?	**Wo kann ich ein Fahrrad/ein Moped/ein Dreirad/ein Tandem mieten?**
Please put some air in this tyre.	**Bitte pumpen Sie diesen Reifen auf.**
One of the spokes is broken.	**Eine der Speichen ist kaputt.**
The brake is not working.	**Die Bremse funktioniert nicht.**
Do you have a bicycle with gears?	**Haben Sie ein Rad mit Gangschaltung?**

The saddle is too high/too low.	**Der Sattel ist zu hoch/zu niedrig.**
Are there any horse-drawn vehicles at this resort?	**Gibt es in diesem Ort Pferdefuhrwerke?**
Will you put the roof down please?	**Würden Sie bitte das Verdeck herunterlassen?**
Will you take the children on the driver's box?	**Dürfen die Kinder auf dem Kutschbock sitzen?**
Are the cable cars working?	**Sind die Seilbahnen in Betrieb?**
Is there a chair-lift?	**Gibt es einen Sessellift?**
Please adjust the safety bar for me.	**Bitte, verstellen Sie den Sicherheitsriegel für mich.**
Do they run frequently?	**Fahren sie häufig?**
How high is the upper station?	**Wie hoch ist die oberste Station?**
Can I walk down?	**Kann ich zu Fuss hinunterkommen?**
Do you sell season tickets?	**Verkaufen Sie Zeitkarten?**

VOCABULARY

bicycle pump	**die Fahrradpumpe**
carrier	**der Gepäckträger**
chain	**die Fahrradkette**
crossbar	**die Fahrradstange**
donkey	**der Esel**
handlebars	**die Lenkstange**
harness	**das Geschirr**
lamp	**die Lampe**

Travelling

mudguard	**der Kotflügel**
pedal	**das Pedal**
rear light	**das Rücklicht**
ski-lift	**der Ski-Lift**
skis	**die Skier**
sledge	**der Schlitten**
toboggan	**der Rodelschlitten**
whip	**die Peitsche**

Walking About

IN TOWN

Is this the main shopping street?	**Ist dies die Hauptgeschäftsstrasse?**
Where is the town hall/police station?	**Wo ist das Rathaus/das Polizeirevier?**
Can you direct me to the Tourist Office?	**Wie komme ich zum Fremdenverkehrsbüro?**
In what part of the town are the theatres/nightclubs?	**In welchem Stadtteil sind die Theater/die Nachtklubs?**
Can I get there by bus/by underground/on foot?	**Kann ich mit dem Bus/mit der U-Bahn/zu Fuss dahinkommen?**
Where is the nearest station/stop/taxi rank?	**Wo ist der nächste Bahnhof/die nächste Haltestelle/der nächste Taxistand?**
Is there a market in the town?	**Gibt es einen Markt in der Stadt?**
What day is market day?	**An welchem Tag ist Markttag?**
Is the business centre near?	**Ist das Geschäftszentrum in der Nähe?**

Must one cross at the traffic lights?	**Muss man bei der Verkehrsampel die Strasse kreuzen?**
Do pedestrians have right of way here?	**Haben Fussgänger hier das Vorrecht?**
Is there a public toilet near?	**Gibt es öffentliche Toiletten in der Nähe?**

VOCABULARY

castle	**das Schloss**
cathedral	**der Dom**
cemetery	**der Friedhof**
church	**die Kirche**
city centre	**die Stadtmitte**
concert hall	**die Konzerthalle**
courts	**die Gerichtsgebäude**
docks	**die Docks**
exhibition	**die Ausstellung**
factory	**die Fabrik**
fortress	**die Festung**
fountain	**der Springbrunnen**
Government buildings	**die Regierungsgebäude**
gardens	**die Gärten**
harbour	**der Hafen**
lake	**der See**
monastery	**das Kloster**
museum	**das Museum**
monument	**das Denkmal**
old town	**die Altstadt**
opera house	**Das Opernhaus**
palace	**der Palast**
park	**der Park**
ruins	**die Ruine**

shopping centre	**das Einkaufszentrum**
stadium	**das Stadion**
statue	**das Standbild**
stock exchange	**die Börse**
subway	**die Unterführung**
traffic lights	**die Verkehrsampel**
tower	**der Turm**
university	**die Universität**
zoo	**der Zoo**

IN THE COUNTRY

May we walk through here?	**Dürfen wir hier durchgehen?**
Is this a public footpath?	**Ist dies ein öffentlicher Fussweg?**
Do I need permission to fish?	**Brauche ich eine Angelerlaubnis?**
Which way is north/southwest/east?	**Welche Richtung ist Nord/Süd/West/Ost?**
Is there a bridge or ford across this stream?	**Gibt es eine Brücke oder eine seichte Stelle über diesen Bach?**
How far is the nearest village?	**Wie weit ist es bis zum nächsten Dorf?**
I am lost. Can you please direct me to ...?	**Ich habe mich verlaufen. Können Sie mir bitte den Weg sagen nach ...?**
Will you please show me the route on this map?	**Würden Sie mir bitte die Strecke auf dieser Karte zeigen?**

VOCABULARY

bird	der Vogel
brook	der Bach
cliff	der Felsen
cottage	das kleine Landhaus
cow	die Kuh
dog	der Hund
farm	der Bauernhof
field	das Feld
footpath	der Fusspfad
forest	der Wald
heath	die Heide
hill	der Hügel
horse	das Pferd
goat	die Ziege
inn	das Wirtshaus
lake	der See
marsh	die Marsch
moorland	das Heideland
mountain	der Berg
orchard	der Obstgarten
peak	die Spitze
pond	der Teich
river	der Fluss
sea	die See
sheep	das Schaf
spring	die Quelle
stream	der Bach
swamp	der Sumpf
tree	der Baum
valley	das Tal
village	das Dorf
vineyard	der Weinberg
waterfall	der Wasserfall
well	der Brunnen

Motoring

At the Frontier

Here is my registration book.	**Hier ist mein Kraftfahrzeugschein.**
my green card insurance.	**meine grüne Versicherungskarte.**
my driving licence.	**mein Führerschein.**
I have an international licence.	**Ich habe einen internationalen Führerschein.**
This is a translation of my British licence.	**Dies ist eine Übersetzung meines britischen Führerscheins.**
This is a self-drive car. Here are the documents.	**Dies ist ein Mietauto. Hier sind die Papiere.**
Do you want to open the boot?	**Wollen Sie den Kofferraum öffnen?**
I arrived today.	**Ich bin heute angekommen.**
I am staying for two weeks.	**Ich bleibe zwei Wochen.**
We are passing through on the way to Italy.	**Wir sind auf der Durchreise nach Italien.**
Does this customs post close at night?	**Ist dieses Zollamt abends geschlossen?**
Do you sell petrol coupons?	**Verkaufen Sie Benzincoupons?**
Shall I leave my engine running?	**Soll ich den Motor laufenlassen?**
Do you want me to stop the engine?	**Soll ich den Motor abstellen?**

44

On the Road

German roads are classified as follows:

Europastrasse	International road	E4
Autobahn	Motorway	BAB
Bundesstrasse	First-class main road	B5
Landesstrasse	Second-class main road	L162
Kreisstrasse	District road	K27

Autobahns are excellent and travel on them is free. There are good service areas and fine restaurants which are licensed. National and departmental roads will go through towns and villages which you would miss on the autobahn. Country roads are narrow and picturesque and are perfect if you are not in a hurry and want to absorb the atmosphere of the region through which you are travelling. On mountain roads give precedence to the car coming uphill. On some roads chains are obligatory in bad weather. There is no speed limit on the autobahns.

Can you tell me how to get to Salzburg?	**Können Sie mir sagen, wie ich nach Salzburg komme?**
How many kilometres is it?	**Wieviele Kilometer sind es?**
Is it a good road?	**Ist die Strasse gut?**
Is it hilly/flat/straight/winding?	**Ist die Strasse hügelig/flach/gerade/kurvenreich?**
What is the speed limit on this section?	**Was ist die Geschwindigkeitsbegrenzung auf dieser Strecke?**
Will you point out the route on this map, please?	**Würden Sir mir bitte die Strecke auf dieser Karte zeigen?**
I am sorry I have no change.	**Es tut mir leid. Ich habe kein Kleingeld.**

How far is it to the next petrol station?	**Wie weit ist es bis zur nächsten Tankstelle?**
I want twenty-five litres, please.	**Ich möchte fünfundzwanzig Liter, bitte.**
Give me 20 Marks' worth.	**Geben Sie mir bitte für zwanzig Mark.**
Fill her up, please.	**Bitte volltanken.**
Please check the oil and water.	**Kontrollieren Sie bitte Ölstand und Wasser.**
I need some air in the tyres.	**Bitte, pumpen Sie die Reifen auf.**
I think the windscreen fluid needs topping up.	**Ich glaube, das Windschutz-scheibenwasser muss aufgefüllt werden.**
Have you any distilled water for the battery?	**Haben Sie destilliertes Wasser für die Batterie?**
Please clean the windscreen.	**Würden Sie bitte die Windschutzscheibe reinigen.**
Have you any paper towels?	**Haben Sie Papierhandtücher?**
Have you got a carwash?	**Haben Sie eine Autowäsche?**
Do you sell yellow filters for the headlights?	**Verkaufen Sie gelbe Filter für die Scheinwerfer?**
Can I park here?	**Kann ich hier parken?**
Where is the nearest car park?	**Wo ist der nächste Parkplatz?**

Trouble with the Police

Usually the police are polite and helpful to visitors, but they are more likely to be so if you appear friendly and cooperative. A few phrases in their language can sometimes work miracles.

I'm sorry. I did not see your signal.	**Es tut mir leid. Ich habe Ihr Zeichen nicht gesehen.**
I thought I had right of way.	**Ich dachte, ich hatte Vorfahrt.**
I apologize. I won't do it again.	**Entschuldigen Sie bitte. Ich werde das nicht wiedertun.**
Here is my name and address.	**Hier sind mein Name und meine Adresse.**
This is my passport.	**Dies is mein Pass.**
Do I have to pay a fine?	**Muss ich eine Geldstrafe zahlen?**
How much?	**Wieviel?**
I haven't got any cash on me. Can I settle up at a police station?	**Ich habe kein Bargeld bei mir. Kann ich es auf dem Polizeirevier erledigen?**
Thank you for your courtesy.	**Vielen Dank für Ihre Gefälligkeit.**

Car Rental

I want to hire a small car.	**Ich möchte ein kleines Auto mieten.**
a family saloon.	**ein Familienauto mieten.**
a large car.	**ein grosses Auto mieten.**
a sports car.	**einen Sportswagen mieten.**
a van.	**einen Lieferwagen mieten.**

Motoring

I shall need it for . . . days.	**Ich brauche es für . . . Tage.**
How much is the daily charge?	**Wieviel kostet es pro Tag?**
Is it cheaper by the week?	**Ist eine Wochenrate billiger?**
Does that include mileage and insurance?	**Sind Kilometergeld und Versicherung einbegriffen?**
Is that insurance fully comprehensive?	**Ist das eine Vollkaskoversicherung?**
What is the mileage charge?	**Was kostet es pro Kilometer?**
Where do I pick up the car?	**Wo hole ich den Wagen ab?**
Can you bring it to my hotel?	**Können Sie ihn zu meinem Hotel bringen?**
Can I leave it at another town or at the airport?	**Kann ich ihn in einer anderen Stadt oder am Flughafen abliefern?**
Is there a deposit to pay?	**Muss ich eine Summe hinterlegen?**
May I pay with my credit card?	**Kann ich mit meiner Kreditkarte zahlen?**
Will you please check the documents with me?	**Würden Sie bitte die Papiere zusammen mit mir durchprüfen?**
Will you show me the gears and instrument panel?	**Würden Sie mir bitte die Gangschaltung und das Armaturenbrett erklären?**
Is the tank full?	**Ist es vollgetankt?**

Road Signs

Ausfahrt	Exit (from motorway)
Einfahrt	Start (of motorway)

48

Ende	Ends
Durchgangsverkehr	Through traffic
Einbahnstrasse	One-way street
Engstelle	Road narrows
Einordnen	Get in lane
Frostschaden	Road damaged by frost
Fussgänger	Pedestrians
Gefährlich	Dangerous
Gegenverkehr	Two-way traffic
Halt. Polizei	Stop. Police
Hupen verboten	Sounding your horn forbidden
Kein Zutritt	No entry
Lawinengefahr	Avalanche area
LKW	For heavy vehicles
Nicht überholen	Overtaking forbidden
Parken verboten	No parking
PKW	For private cars
Radweg kreuzt	Cycle crossing
Rechts fahren	Keep right
Sackgasse	Cul-de-sac
Schule	School
Steinschlag	Falling stones
Strassenarbeiten	Roadworks
Umleitung	Diversion
Vorsicht	Caution

Trouble on the Road

OTHER PEOPLE'S

There has been an accident on the road three miles back.	**Da ist ein Unfall passiert. Etwa fünf Kilometer zurück.**
Will you phone the police, please?	**Würden Sie bitte die Polizei anrufen?**
No, I did not see it happen.	**Ich habe nicht gesehen, wie es passiert ist.**
The car registration number was ...	**Das Autokennzeichen ist ...**
I do not think anyone is hurt.	**Ich glaube nicht, dass jemand verletzt ist.**
Someone is badly hurt.	**Jemand ist schwer verletzt.**

YOURS

Are you all right?	**Sind Sie unverletzt?**
My passengers are not hurt.	**Meine Mitfahrer sind nicht verletzt.**
The car is damaged.	**Der Wagen ist beschädigt.**
May I have your insurance details?	**Kann ich die Einzelheiten Ihrer Versicherung haben?**
Your name and address please?	**Ihren Namen und Adresse bitte?**
Will you please fill out this form?	**Würden Sie bitte dieses Formular ausfüllen?**
I think we shall have to call the police.	**Wir müssen wohl die Polizei benachrichtigen.**
Excuse me, would you mind being a witness?	**Verzeihung, würden Sie bitte als Zeuge auftreten?**

It happened because he put his brakes on suddenly.	**Es passierte, weil er plötzlich bremste.**
He came out of a side road without signalling.	**Er kam aus einer Nebenstrasse, ohne ein Zeichen zu geben.**
He tried to overtake on a narrow stretch of road.	**Er versuchte, auf einer engen Strecke zu überholen.**
He turned off without signalling.	**Er bog ab, ohne ein Zeichen zu geben.**
May I explain to someone who understands English?	**Kann ich das jemandem erklären, der Englisch versteht?**

If you are unfortunate enough to have an accident, be sure to get all the details from the other driver involved. Your insurance company will have provided you with an accident report form. Fill it up on the spot with the help of the other driver. Above all, keep cool.

Breakdown

If you have a breakdown put out the red triangle behind the car at once or you may be penalized. Get your car off the road if possible.

Thank you for stopping. I am in trouble. Will you help me?	**Vielen Dank, dass Sie anhalten. Ich bin in Nöten. Würden Sie mir bitte helfen?**
My car has broken down.	**Mein Wagen hat eine Panne.**
Will you tell the next garage or breakdown service vehicle if you see one.	**Würden Sie bitte die nächste Reparaturwerkstatt benachrichtigen oder die ADAC Strassenwacht, wenn Sie eine sehen.**

Motoring

Will you please telephone a garage for me?	**Würden Sie bitte eine Reparaturwerkstatt für mich anrufen?**
Can you give me a lift to the next telephone?	**Könnten Sie mich bis zum nächsten Telefon mitnehmen?**
Can you send a breakdown truck?	**Könnten Sie bitte einen Abschleppwagen schicken?**
I am five kilometres from the last entry.	**Ich bin fünf Kilometer von der letzten Einfahrt entfernt.**
I am three kilometres from Bonn on the Autobahn.	**Ich bin auf der Autobahn drei Kilometer von Bonn entfernt.**
How long will you be?	**Wie lange wird es dauern?**

Repairs

There's something wrong with the engine.	**Der Motor ist nicht in Ordnung.**
The clutch is slipping.	**Die Kupplung rutscht.**
There is a noise from the ...	**Da ist ein Geräusch von ...**
The brakes are not working.	**Die Bremsen funktionieren nicht.**
The water system is leaking.	**Die Wasserpumpe ist undicht.**
My fan belt is broken.	**Der Keilriemen ist kaputt.**
I've got a flat tyre.	**Ich habe eine Reifenpanne.**
The electrical system isn't working.	**Die elektrische Anlage funktioniert nicht.**

The engine is overheating.	**Der Motor ist überhitzt.**
The car won't start.	**Der Wagen springt nicht an.**
What is the matter?	**Was ist los?**
Is it broken?	**Ist es kaputt?**
burnt out?	**ausgebrannt?**
disconnected?	**losgelöst?**
jammed?	**blockiert?**
leaking?	**undicht?**
Has it short-circuited?	**Hat er Kurzschluss?**
Do I need a new part?	**Brauche ich ein Ersatzteil?**
Is there a Ford agent in town?	**Gibt es eine Ford-Vertretung in der Stadt?**
Can you send for the part?	**Können Sie das Ersatzteil kommenlassen?**
Is it serious?	**Ist es schlimm?**
How long will it take to repair?	**Wie lange wird die Reparatur dauern?**
Can I hire another car?	**Kann ich einen anderen Wagen mieten?**
What will it cost?	**Wieviel kostet es?**
I will get the part flown from Britain.	**Ich werde das Ersatzteil aus England fliegen lassen.**
Your mechanic has been very kind. I would like to tip him.	**Ihr Autoschlosser war sehr gefällig. Ich möchte ihm ein Trinkgeld geben.**

VOCABULARY

battery	**die Batterie**

brakes	**die Bremsen**
brake lining	**der Bremsbelag**
bulbs	**die Glühbirnen**
carburettor	**der Vergaser**
clutch	**die Kuppelung**
cooling system	**die Kühlung**
dip switch	**der Abblendschalter**
dynamo	**die Lichtmaschine**
distributor	**der Verteiler**
electrical system	**die elektrische Anlage**
exhaust pipe	**das Auspuffrohr**
fan	**der Ventilator**
filter	**der Filter**
fuel pump	**die Benzinpumpe**
fuel tank	**der Benzintank**
gears	**die Gänge**
generator	**der Generator**
hand brake	**die Handbremse**
headlights	**die Scheinwerfer**
heating system	**die Heizung**
horn	**die Hupe**
ignition	**die Zündung**
indicator	**der Blinker**
lubrication system	**das Schmiersystem**
radiator	**der Kühler**
reflector	**der Reflektor**
seat	**der Sitz**
silencer	**der Lautdämpfer**
sparking plug	**die Zündkerze**
suspension	**die Federung**
transmission	**das Getriebe**
wheels	**die Räder**
windscreen wipers	**die Scheibenwischer**

A Place to Stay

There are places to suit every budget level in German-speaking Europe, from the great luxury palaces of the famous spas to the country inn with rooms to let. If you have not booked a hotel in advance, ask at the tourist office, **das Fremdenverkehrsbüro**, of each town. They will help you to find a place within your price range. If you don't want to stay at a hotel there are villas and country cottages, camping sites and rooms in private houses. The standards of comfort vary considerably, but the German-speaking people provide good, clean accommodation at all price levels. The main types of places with accommodation are:

Hotel	classified from luxurious to simple pension
Rasthaus	wayside lodge, motel
Gasthaus	an inn
Jugendherberge	youth hostel
Ferienwohnung	furnished flat

Private houses also advertise rooms with signs saying **'Zimmer frei'**.

Hotels and Pensions

Finding a Room

I am travelling with the ... travel agency.	**Ich reise mit der ... Reisegesellschaft.**
Here is my hotel coupon.	**Hier ist mein Hotelkoupon.**
My room is already reserved.	**Mein Zimmer ist schon reserviert.**
I am travelling independently.	**Ich reise allein.**
Will a porter bring my luggage in?	**Wird der Hoteldiener mein Gepäck hereinbringen?**
Can I leave my car here?	**Kann ich meinen Wagen hier stehenlassen?**
Is there a car park?	**Gibt es hier einen Parkplatz?**
Are you the receptionist/ concierge/manager?	**Sind Sie der Empfangschef/ der Portier/der Manager?**
Have you a single/double/three-bedded room?	**Haben Sie ein Einbettzimmer/ein Doppelzimmer/ein Dreibettzimmer?**
with a full-size bath and separate toilet?	**mit Bad und Toilette getrennt?**
with a bath or shower?	**mit Bad oder Dusche?**
with a balcony?	**mit Balkon?**
looking over the front/back?	**mit Blick nach vorne/nach hinten?**
How much is it per day?	**Wieviel kostet es pro Tag?**
Is there a reduction for a longer stay/for children?	**Gibt es eine Preisermässigung für einen längeren Aufenthalt/für Kinder?**

Are there special mealtimes for children?	**Gibt es separate Essenszeiten für Kinder?**
I don't want to pay more than ... Marks per day.	**Ich möchte nicht mehr als ... Mark pro Tag ausgeben.**
Have you anything cheaper?	**Haben Sie etwas Billigeres?**
Do I have to fill in a visitor's card?	**Muss ich ein Anmeldungsformular ausfüllen?**
Here is my passport.	**Hier ist mein Pass.**
How long will you keep it?	**Wie lange werden Sie ihn brauchen?**
I'd like to go up to my room right away.	**Ich möchte gern sofort auf mein Zimmer gehen.**
Will you send up the luggage?	**Würden Sie bitte das Gepäck hinaufbringen lassen?**
This case is for room 3 and that one for Number 12.	**Diesser Koffer ist für Zimmer drei und der für Zimmer zwölf.**
May I have the room key?	**Kann ich bitte den Zimmerschlüssel haben?**
Is the key in the door?	**Steckt der Schlüssel in der Tür?**
Where is the lift? Do I work it myself?	**Wo ist der Fahrstuhl? Kann ich ihn selbst bedienen?**
Do you do bed and breakfast/ demi pension?	**Kann man hier Übernachtung und Frühstück/Halbpension bekommen?**

Accommodation

Can you put all the extras on my bill?	**Würden Sie bitte alle Extrakosten mit auf meine Rechnung setzen?**
Is there a post box in the hotel?	**Gibt es einen Briefkasten im Hotel?**
Can you get the daily papers for me?	**Könnten Sie mir die Tageszeitungen besorgen?**

Moving In

This room is too small/large/noisy/dark/high up.	**Dieses Zimmer ist zu klein/gross/laut/dunkel/liegt zu hoch.**
Haven't you got a double bed?	**Haben Sie kein Doppelbett?**
Can you please make the twin beds into one double?	**Würden Sie bitte aus den Einzelbetten ein Doppelbett machen?**
I shall need another pillow. another blanket. another clothes hanger. some writing paper.	**Ich brauche noch ein Kissen. noch eine Decke. noch einen Kleiderbügel. etwas Schreibpapier.**
The bedside light is not working. The bulb is broken.	**Die Nachttischlampe funktioniert nicht. Die Birne ist kaputt.**
Which is the hot/cold tap?	**Wo ist der Wasserhahn für heisses/kaltes Wasser?**
Is this the electric razor socket?	**Ist dies die Steckdose für den Rasierapparat?**
What is the voltage here?	**Welche Stromspannung haben Sie hier?**
My plug won't fit.	**Mein Stecker passt nicht.**

58

Have you got an adaptor?	**Haben Sie einen Zwischenstecker?**
Is there an electrician in the village?	**Gibt es einen Elektriker im Dorf?**
Is there a hotel laundry?	**Gibt es eine Hotelwäscherei?**
Are there facilities for washing and ironing?	**Gibt es hier eine Möglichkeit zum Waschen und Bügeln?**
The blind is stuck.	**Die Jalousie klemmt.**
Will you bring a bottle of drinking water?	**Würden Sie mir bitte eine Flasche Trinkwasser bringen?**
Can I leave valuables in the hotel safe?	**Kann ich Wertgegenstände im Hoteltresor lassen?**
What time is breakfast/lunch/dinner?	**Wann gibt es Frühstück/Mittagessen/Abendessen?**
Do you serve breakfast in bed?	**Servieren Sie Frühstück aufs Zimmer?**
Does the hotel do packed lunches?	**Können wir hier statt Mittagessen ein Lunchpaket bekommen?**

Small Hotels and Pensions

Do you have set times for meals?	**Haben Sie bestimmte Essenszeiten?**
May I have a towel and soap?	**Kann ich bitte Handtuch und Seife haben?**
At what time do you lock the front door at night?	**Wann wird die Haustür nachts abgeschlossen?**
May I have a key?	**Könnte ich einen Schlüssel haben?**

Accommodation

Is it all right to leave the car in the street?	**Kann ich meinen Wagen auf der Strasse stehenlassen?**
Will our things be safe?	**Sind unsere Sachen hier sicher?**
Where is the nearest garage?	**Wo ist die nächste Garage?**

Rooms in Private Houses

Do you have a room free?	**Haben Sie ein Zimmer frei?**
You don't do breakfast?	**Sie geben kein Frühstück?**
Is there a café nearby?	**Gibt es ein Café in der Nähe?**
Would you like me to pay now?	**Soll ich jetzt bezahlen?**
At what time will it be convenient to use the bathroom?	**Wann darf ich das Badezimmer benutzen?**
Do I need to tell you if I have a bath?	**Muss ich Bescheid sagen, wenn ich ein Bad nehmen möchte?**
Could you wake us in the morning?	**Würden Sie uns bitte morgen früh wecken?**
Is there a lounge?	**Gibt es hier einen Aufenthaltsraum?**
Shall I lock my room?	**Soll ich mein Zimmer abschliessen?**

Paying the Bill

May I have my bill, please?	**Könnte ich bitte meine Rechnung haben?**
Will you prepare my bill for first thing tomorrow?	**Würden Sie bitte meine Rechnung für morgenfrüh fertigmachen?**

I think there is a mistake.	**Ich glaube, da stimmt etwas nicht.**
I don't understand this item.	**Ich verstehe diesen Posten nicht.**
May I pay by cheque? Yes, I have a Eurocheque card.	**Kann ich Ihnen einen Scheck geben? Ja, ich habe eine Euro-Scheckkarte.**
Do you accept credit cards?	**Kann ich mit Kreditkarte bezahlen?**
Is service included?	**Ist Bedienung einbegriffen?**
Is VAT included?	**Ist Mehrwertsteuer einbegriffen?**
May I have a receipt please?	**Könnte ich bitte eine Quittung haben?**
Please forward my mail to ...	**Bitte, schicken Sie mir meine Post nach ...**
We have enjoyed ourselves very much.	**Es hat uns sehr gut gefallen.**
May I have one of your leaflets?	**Könnte ich eine Ihrer Broschüren haben?**

Vocabulary

bar	**die Bar**
barman	**der Barmann**
bed	**das Bett**
chair	**der Stuhl**
chambermaid	**das Zimmermädchen**
children's playground	**der Kinderspielplatz**
discotheque	**die Diskothek**
door	**die Tür**

Accommodation

hall	**die Halle**
lift	**der Fahrstuhl**
lounge	**der Aufenthaltsraum**
light switch	**der Lichtschalter**
luggage porter	**der Hausdiener**
manager	**der Geschäftsführer**
night club	**der Nachtklub**
playground	**der Spielplatz**
radio	**das Radio**
restaurant	**das Restaurant**
stairs	**die Treppe**
swimming pool	**das Schwimmbad**
telephone operator	**der Telefonist**
waiter	**der Kellner**
waitress	**die Kellnerin**
wardrobe	**der Schrank**
window	**das Fenster**

Catering for Yourself

Villas and Apartments

I have booked a villa/apartment.	**Ich habe eine Villa/Ferienwohnung reserviert.**
Here is my voucher.	**Hier ist mein Gutschein.**
Will you please show me around?	**Würden Sie mir bitte alles zeigen?**
Where is the light switch/power point/fuse box?	**Wo ist der Lichtschalter/die Steckdose/die Sicherungen?**
Do all the outside doors lock?	**Sind alle äusseren Türen verschliessbar?**
How do the shutters work?	**Wie funktionieren die Fensterläden?**
Will you show me the hot water system?	**Können Sie mir bitte die Heisswasseranlage zeigen?**
Where is the mains valve?	**Wo ist der Haupthahn?**
Is there mains gas?	**Gibt es Anschlussgas?**
Are gas cylinders delivered?	**Werden Gaszylinder geliefert?**
At what time does the house help come?	**Um wieviel Uhr kommt die Hausgehilfin?**
Can we have three sets of house keys?	**Könnten wir bitte drei Satz Hausschlüssel haben?**
When is the rubbish collected?	**Wann wird der Abfall abgeholt?**
Are the shops nearby?	**Gibt es Geschäfte in der Nähe?**

Catering for Yourself

Where is the bus stop/station?	**Wo ist die Bushaltestelle/der Bahnhof?**
Have you a map of the area?	**Haben Sie einen Plan der Umgebung?**

Camping

Have you got a site free?	**Haben Sie einen Platz frei?**
Do you rent out bungalows? tents? cooking equipment?	**Vermieten Sie Bungalows? Zelte? Kochausrüstungen?**
Where are the toilet and washing facilities? cooking facilities?	**Wo sind hier Toiletten und Waschräume? Kochgelegenheiten?**
How much does it cost per night?	**Wieviel kostet es pro Nacht?**
Can I put my tent here?	**Kann ich mein Zelt hier aufschlagen?**
Is there room for a trailer?	**Ist hier Platz für einen Wohnwagen?**
Is there a night guard?	**Gibt es eine Nachtwache?**
Where is the camp shop? the restaurant? the nearest shopping centre?	**Wo ist das Camping-Geschäft? das Restaurant? das nächste Einkaufszentrum?**
At what time do we have to vacate the site?	**Um wieviel Uhr müssen wir den Platz räumen?**
Where is the drinking tap?	**Wo ist der Trinkwasserhahn?**

Vocabulary

barbecue	**das Barbecue**
basin	**die Schüssel**
bucket	**der Eimer**
camping gas	**das Campinggas**
frame tent	**das Giebelzelt**
grill	**der Grill**
guy ropes	**die Halteseile**
ice-bucket	**der Eiskübel**
insecticide	**das Insektenmittel**
knife	**das Messer**
mosquito repellant	**das Moskitomittel**
penknife	**das Taschenmesser**
sleeping bag	**der Schlafsack**
spade	**der Spaten**
stove	**der Kocher**
tent	**das Zelt**
tent peg	**der Hering/Zeltpflock**
waterproof sheet	**der Zeltboden**

Youth Hostelling

Is there a youth hostel in this town?	**Gibt es eine Jugendherberge in dieser Stadt?**
Have you room for tonight?	**Haben Sie ein Bett frei für heute nacht?**
We are members of the Youth Hostels Association.	**Wir sind Mitglieder des Jugendherbergsvereins.**
What are the house rules?	**Wie sind die Hausregeln?**
How long can we stay?	**Wie lange können wir hier bleiben?**
Is there a youth hostel at ...?	**Gibt es eine Jugendherberge in ...?**

Eating and Drinking

Mealtimes not only offer a chance to satisfy the appetite, but they also provide an intimate glimpse of the life of the places you are visiting. There are the regional specialities to whet the appetite and to reveal something of the character of the local environment. The dishes of north Germany, for example, are different from those of Bavaria. In the former the North Sea and the farms of the plain contribute fresh fish, meat and vegetables. In Bavaria there are endless varieties of sausage to accompany the beer, and in Austria veal and game dishes are available.

Above all, mealtimes provide an opportunity to watch the fascinating drama of people: the farmer at the village beer cellars, the families at Sunday lunch, the German holiday-makers at their resorts. Different types of restaurant satisfy different tastes and there is a wide variety.

At beerhalls (**Bierhallen**) you will get food as well as beer. At a **Café** or **Konditorei** there are coffee and cakes. **Raststätte** are wayside restaurants. **Weinstuben** are wine bars where hot food is served, and restaurants of various nationalities abound everywhere.

Can you recommend a good restaurant?	**Empfehlen Sie mir bitte ein gutes Restaurant.**
one that is not too expensive?	**ein nicht zu teures Restaurant.**
a typical restaurant of the region?	**ein typisches Restaurant für diese Gegend.**
one with music?	**ein Restaurant mit musikalischen Darbietungen.**
a four-star establishment?	**ein vier-Stern-Restaurant.**

a Chinese/Indian/Arabic/ Italian/French restaurant?	**ein chinesisches/indisches/ arabisches/italienisches/ französisches Restaurant?**
Is there a good snack bar nearby?	**Gibt es eine gute Schnellimbisshalle in der Nähe?**
Where can I find a self-service restaurant?	**Wo gibt es ein Selbstbedienungs- restaurant?**
Do I need to reserve a table?	**Muss man einen Tisch reservieren?**
I'd like a table for two at nine o'clock, please.	**Ich möchte einen Tisch für zwei Personen für neun Uhr, bitte.**
not too near the door. in the corner. away from the kitchen.	**nicht so dicht an der Tür. in der Ecke. nicht bei der Küche.**

At the Restaurant

A table for four, please.	**Einen Tisch für vier Personen, bitte.**
Is this our table?	**Ist dies unser Tisch?**
This table will do fine.	**Dieser Tisch gefällt mir.**
The tablecloth is dirty.	**Das Tischtuch ist schmutzig.**
The table is unsteady.	**Der Tisch wackelt.**
The ashtray is missing.	**Hier ist kein Aschenbecher.**
May I see the menu?	**Könnte ich die Speisekarte sehen, bitte?**
We will have an aperitif while we look at the menu.	**Wir möchten einen Aperitif, während wir die Speisekarte studieren.**
Please bring the wine list.	**Bitte, bringen Sie die Weinliste.**
Have you a set menu?	**Haben Sie ein Tagesmenü?**
What do you recommend today?	**Was können Sie uns heute empfehlen?**
What does it consist of?	**Woraus besteht es?**
It sounds good. I'll try it.	**Das klingt gut. Ich möchte es probieren.**
The soup is cold. Please warm it up.	**Die Suppe ist kalt. Bitte, wärmen Sie sie auf.**
This fork is dirty. May I have a clean one?	**Die Gabel ist schmutzig. Könnte ich eine saubere haben?**
Will you call our waiter?	**Würden Sie bitte unseren Ober rufen?**

We did not order this.	**Wir haben dies nicht bestellt.**
I'd like to speak to the Head Waiter.	**Ich möchte den Oberkellner sprechen.**
My compliments to the chef.	**Ich gratuliere dem Küchenchef.**
It's very good.	**Es schmeckt sehr gut.**
Have you any house wine?	**Haben Sie einen Hauswein?**
I'd like a half bottle.	**Ich möchte eine halbe Flasche.**
Which is the local wine?	**Welcher ist der hiesige Wein?**
This wine is corked.	**Dieser Wein schmeckt korkig.**
The children will share a portion.	**Die Kinder teilen sich eine Portion.**
May we have some water?	**Könnten wir Wasser haben?**
Have you any mineral water?	**Haben Sie Mineralwasser?**
Have you a high chair for the child?	**Haben Sie einen Kinderstuhl?**
Will you please bring some cushions?	**Würden Sie bitte ein paar Kissen bringen?**
Where are the toilets?	**Wo sind die Toiletten?**
Is service included?	**Ist Bedienung inbegriffen?**

The Menu

Menus will vary from place to place and will feature different regional dishes. In the north and in Hanseatic towns, meat and green vegetables are an important part of the diet. Mutton is a common ingredient and so are the salt water fish of the North Sea. In the Rhineland, cakes and bread of various kinds are a speciality and in the Black Forest game is plentiful. Bavaria specializes in sausages which are washed down with copious draughts of the excellent Bavarian beer.

Restaurants offer fixed price menus (**Gedecke**) and à la carte. Mealtimes usually begin at midday and 1900 hours. There is often a service charge of 15% on the total bill.

Starters

Aal in Gelee	jellied eels
Appetithäppchen	canapés
Fleischpastete	meat pâté
Gänseleberpastete	goose liver pâté
Bismarckhering	soused herring
Matjeshering	young salted herring
Hoppel Poppel	scrambled egg with sausages
Käsehappen	cheese straws
Königinpastete	vol-au-vent with mushrooms and meat
Lachs	salmon
Muscheln	mussels
Pilze	mushrooms
Räucheraal	smoked eel

Russische Eier	egg mayonnaise
Sardellen	anchovies
Sardinen	sardines
Schinken	ham
Schinkenrolle mit Spargel	ham rolled around asparagus
Strammer Max	minced pork with egg and onions

Soups

Aalsuppe	eel soup
Bauernsuppe	sausage and cabbage soup
Bohnensuppe	bean soup
Fischbeuschelsuppe	fish roe soup
Fridattensuppe	soup with strips of pancake
Frühlingssuppe	fresh vegetable soup
Griessknockerlsuppe	semolina dumpling soup
Gulaschsuppe	goulash soup
Hühnerbrühe	chicken broth
Knödelsuppe	dumpling soup
Königinsuppe	beef soup with sour cream and almonds
Kraftbrühe mit Eiern	consommé with egg
Leberknödlsuppe	liver meatball soup
Nudelsuppe	noodle soup
Pichelsteiner Eintopf	meat and vegetable stew
Schildkrötensuppe	turtle soup

71

Eating and Drinking

Serbische Bohnensuppe	Serbian bean soup
Tomatensuppe	tomato soup
Zwiebelsuppe	onion soup
Backerbsensuppe	broth with croutons
Kaltschale	cold fruit soup
Labskaus	lamb and potato stew

Fish

Fisch gedämpft mit Senf-Sauce	steamed fish with mustard sauce
Blauer Aal	blued eel
Blaue Forelle	blued trout
Grüner Aal mit Gurkensalat	green eel with cucumber salad
Rochen mit Sauerkraut	skate with sauerkraut
Fische mit Kümmelkraut	fish with cabbage and carraway seeds
Schellfish nach Hamburger Art	haddock Hamburg style
Hechtauflauf	pike and cauliflower cheese
Hummer in Weissbier	lobster cooked in beer

Meat

Bauernomelett	bacon and onion omelette
Bauernschmaus	sauerkraut with pork, bacon and sausages
Bierwurst	large bland sausage
Blutwurst	black pudding

Bockwurst	large frankfurter
Bündnerfleisch	finely sliced smoked meat
Deutsches Beefsteak	beefburger
Eisbein	pig's knuckle
Filetsteak	steak
blutig	rare
mittel	medium
durchgebraten	well done
Fleischkäse	type of sausage
Geschnetzeltes	veal cubes in wine sauce
Gefüllte Kalbsbrust	stuffed veal
Geselchtes	salted pork
Gulasch	meat stewed in paprika sauce
Hackbraten	meat loaf
Holsteiner Schnitzel	veal escalope with egg and anchovies
Kasseler Rippenspeer	smoked pork chops
Königsberger Klops	meat balls in caper sauce
Kohlroulade	stuffed cabbage
Rouladen	rolled meat served in sauce
Schlachtplatte	variety of cold meats
Wiener Schnitzel	veal escalope in breadcrumbs

Eating and Drinking

Game and Poultry

Gefüllter Gänsehals	stuffed goose neck
Gänseklein	goose giblets
Gänseleber mit Äpfeln und Zwiebeln	goose liver with apples and onions
Junges Huhn nach Jäger Art	chicken in hunter style
Gebratener Auerhahn	roast capercailzie
Hasenrücken mit Meerrettich	saddle of hare and horseradish
Rehkotelett	venison steak
Gebratene Ente	roast duck
Gebratene Tauben	roast pigeon
Rebhühner mit Sauerkraut	partridge with sauerkraut

Vegetables

Leipziger Allerlei	mixed vegetables in Leipzig style
Gefüllter Kohl	stuffed cabbage
Rotkohl	red cabbage
Kartoffelpuffer	potato pancakes
Grüne Bohnen mit Speck	green beans with bacon
Wachsbohnen mit Birnen	butter beans with pears
Himmel und Erde	apples and potatoes (literally 'heaven and earth')
Kürbisbrei mit Käse	pumpkin and cheese

Desserts

Apfelstrudel	pastry filled with apples, nuts and raisins
Berliner	doughnut
Eis	ice-cream
Erdbeer	strawberry
Karamel	caramel
Mokka	coffee
Schokoladen	chocolate
Bienenstich	honey and almond cake
Gugelhupf	ring-shaped cake with raisins and almonds
Hefekranz	ring-shaped yeast cake
Kaiserschmarren	shredded pancake with raisins and syrup
Mohrenkopf	chocolate pastry with whipped cream
Palatschinken	pancakes
Sachertorte	chocolate cake with apricot jam
Hazelnussmandelmakronen	hazelnut macaroons
Quark mit Erdbeeren	cottage cheese with strawberries
Fürst Pückler Rahmbombe	iced bombe

Drinks

The most usual drink in German-speaking countries is beer
and most towns have their own breweries which produce a
light, lager-type beer. You can get draught beer and it comes
as light or dark. Altbier is a bitter, and Bock, Doppelbock,
Marzen and Starkbier have a higher alcoholic content.
Pilsener is a lager beer with a strong taste of hops and
Weissbier is a very pale variety. Aperitifs are those found
internationally – sherry, vermouth, vodka, gin and tonic, etc.

I would like a light beer please.	**Ich möchte ein Helles, bitte.**
My friend will have a dark beer.	**Mein Freund möchte ein Dunkles.**
Bring a bottle/a glass, please.	**Bringen Sie bitte eine Flasche/ein Glas.**
Have you any gin and tonic?	**Haben Sie Gin mit Tonic?**
Not too much tonic, thank you.	**Nicht zu viel Tonic, bitte.**
Some ice and lemon, please.	**Etwas Eis und Zitrone, bitte.**
I'd like a Scotch on the rocks/ with plain water/with soda.	**Ich möchte einen Scotch on the rocks/mit Wasser/mit Sodawasser.**
Have you any non-alcoholic drinks?	**Haben Sie alkoholfreie Getränke?**

Wine

German wines are excellent and are mostly grown in the
Rhine and Moselle valleys. German wines sometimes have
sugar added when the summer has not allowed the grapes to
ripen naturally. When this happens the labels bear the word
verbessert. German wine labels also carry words that denote
the ripeness and quality of the grapes when picked.

Spätlese means that they have been gathered after the normal harvest and that the wine will be dry.
Auslese means that the wine is made from selected bunches of grapes and the wine will be on the dry side.
Beerenauslese indicates overripe grapes and the wine is slightly sweet.
Trockenbeerenauslese are wines from grapes that are becoming raisins and the wine is sweet.

The main wine-growing areas in Germany are Rheingau, between Wiesbaden and Rudesheim on the east bank of the Rhine, which produces Johannisberger wine; Rheinhessen, further south, the home of the Liebfraumilch, and Franconia, where dry, full-bodied wine is made. One of the best wines of the region is Steinwein, which is bottled in the traditional squat bottle called **Bocksbeutel**.

Moselle wines come from the Riesling grape and among the most famous are Bernkastel and Piesport. Palatinate, which lies along the borders of Alsace and Lorraine, also produces some fine wines from Riesling grapes. Germany also excels in sparkling white wines known as Sekt.

In Austria there are white wines similar to those of the Rhine and the Italian Tyrol. The most famous Austrian wine, however, is probably Gumpold Kirchener, produced south of Vienna. Other wines are Nassberger, Wiener and Grinzinger.

Soft Drinks

May we have some tea, please?	**Könnten wir bitte Tee haben?**
a pot of tea?	**eine Kanne Tee haben?**
a lemon tea?	**Zitronentee haben?**
China/Indian tea?	**chinesischen/indischen Tee haben?**
coffee with milk/cream?	**Kaffee mit Milch/Sahne haben?**

Eating and Drinking

a black coffee?	**Schwarzen Kaffee haben?**
iced coffee?	**Eiskaffee haben?**
Have you any lemonade?	**Haben Sie Zitronenlimonade?**
an orange juice with soda water?	**einen Orangensprudel?**
a glass of cold milk?	**ein Glas kalte Milch?**
I'd like a long cool fruit juice with plenty of ice.	**Ich möchte ein grosses Glas Fruchtsaft mit viel Eis.**
Have you a straw?	**Haben Sie einen Strohhalm?**
Do you make milk shakes?	**Haben Sie Milchmixgetränke?**
Have you a bottle with a screw top?	**Haben Sie eine Flasche mit einem Schraubdeckel?**

Vocabulary

beeftea	**die Bouillon**
canned beer	**das Kannenbier**
chocolate	**die Schokolade**
cordial	**der Fruchtsaft**
cup	**die Tasse**
ginger ale	**das Ingwerbier**
lager	**das Lagerbier**
syphon	**der Siphon**
tonic	**Tonic**
tumbler	**der Becher**

Shopping

Buying Food

Eating out is fun, but so is buying food in the various types of food shops and markets. The Germans set great store by freshness and quality, and buying food is an important operation involving much discussion about the product.

At the Butcher's

What kind of meat is that?	**Welche Fleischsorte ist das?**
What do you call that cut?	**Wie nennt man das Stück Fleisch?**
I'd like some steaks, please.	**Ich möchte ein paar Steaks.**
How much does that weigh?	**Wieviel wiegt das?**
Will you please trim off the fat?	**Würden Sie bitte das Fett wegschneiden?**
Will you take the meat off the bone?	**Würden Sie bitte den Knochen herausschneiden?**
Will you mince it?	**Würden Sie es bitte durch den Wolf drehen?**
Please cut it in thin slices/in thick slices.	**Bitte, schneiden Sie es in dünne Scheiben/in dicke Scheiben.**
Will you chine the cutlets?	**Würden Sie bitte die Knochen aus den Koteletts schneiden?**
I'll have a little more.	**Ich möchte etwas mehr haben.**
That's too much.	**Das ist zu viel.**

Buying Food

Please put it in a plastic bag. **Tun Sie es bitte in einen
Plastikbeutel.**

Cut it in cubes, please. **In Würfel schneiden bitte.**

beef	**Rindfleisch**
pot roast	**Schmorbraten**
rib	**Rippensteak**
rumpsteak	**Rumpsteak**
filet	**Filet**
roast beef	**Rinderbraten**
sirloin	**Lendenstück**
brains	**das Hirn**
cutlets	**die Koteletten**
cooking fat	**das Speisefett**
escalope	**das Schnitzel**
bacon	**der Speck**
leg of lamb	**die Lammkeule**
shoulder of lamb	**die Lammschulter**
liver	**die Leber**
kidneys	**die Nieren**
tongue	**die Zunge**
pigs' trotters	**die Schweinsfüsse**
knuckle of pork	**das Eisbein**
leg of pork	**die Schweinekeule**
pork chop	**das Schweinekotelett**
sweetbreads	**der Bries**
sausage	**das Würstchen**

At the Fishmonger's

Will you clean the fish? **Würden Sie bitte den Fisch
ausnehmen?**

Please take off the head/tail and fins.	**Bitte, schneiden Sie Kopf/ Schwanz und Flossen ab.**
Have you any shellfish?	**Haben Sie Schalentiere?**
What is the name of that fish?	**Wie heisst dieser Fisch?**

VOCABULARY

anchovies	**die Sardellen**
bass	**der Barsch**
carp	**der Karpfen**
cod	**der Dorsch**
crayfish	**der Flusskrebs**
crab	**der Krebs**
clams	**die Muscheln**
bream	**die Brasse**
eel	**der Aal**
herring	**der Hering**
lobster	**die Languste der Hummer**
oysters	**die Austern**
mullet	**die Meeräsche**
mussels	**die Muscheln**
octopus	**der Tintenfisch**
perch	**der Zander**
pike	**der Hecht**
prawns	**die Garnelen**
plaice	**die Scholle**
salmon	**der Lachs**
squid	**der Tintenfisch**
sardines	**die Sardinen**
sole	**die Seezunge**
trout	**die Forelle**
tunny	**der Thunfisch**
turbot	**der Steinbutt**
whitebait	**der Weissfisch**

At the Delicatessen

What kinds of sausage have you got?	**Welche Wurstarten haben Sie?**
I'd like a mild one/peppery one/one without garlic.	**Ich möchte eine milde Wurst/eine pfeffrige Wurst/eine ohne Knoblauch.**
What kinds of pâté have you?	**Welche Sorten von Paté haben Sie?**
I prefer a coarse pâté/smooth pâté/game pâté.	**Ich möchte eine grobe Paté/eine feine Paté/eine Wildpaté.**
What is the name of that cheese?	**Wie heisst der Käse?**
Have you any goat's cheese?	**Haben Sie Ziegenkäse?**
Do I have to take the whole cheese or will you cut me a piece?	**Muss ich den ganzen Käse kaufen oder schneiden Sie mir ein Stück?**
May I test it for ripeness?	**Darf ich ihn probieren?**
Do you sell breakfast cereals?	**Haben Sie Frühstückcereals?**
Have you any biscuits/tea biscuits?	**Haben Sie Kekse/Teegebäck?**
I'll take a little of each salad.	**Ich möchte ein wenig von jedem Salat.**
Have you a tube of tomato purée?	**Haben Sie Tomatenpuree in der Tube?**
I would like a jar of olives.	**Ich möchte ein Glas Oliven.**

VOCABULARY

dried beef	**das getrocknete Rindfleisch**
garlic sausage	**die Knoblauchwurst**
ham	**der Schinken**
macaroni	**Makaroni**
olives	**die Oliven**
pickles	**Pickles**
Quiche	**Quiche**
spaghetti	**Spaghetti**
smoked fish	**der geräucherte Fisch**
tinned food	**die Konserven**

CHEESES

Allgäuer Bergkäse	mild cheese
Altenburger	goat cheese
Appenzeller	mild cheese
Kümmelkäse	cheese made with caraway seeds
Räucherkäse	smoked cheese
Sahnekäse	cream cheese
Tilsiter	mild cheese
Handkäse	a sharp cheese
Harzerkäse	a cheese from the Harz mountains

At the Greengrocer and Fruiterer's

Is the melon ripe?	**Ist die Melone reif?**
How many will make a kilo?	**Wieviele bekomme ich auf ein Kilo?**
It's for eating tomorrow.	**Wir wollen sie morgen essen.**
Will you please weigh this?	**Würden Sie dies bitte wiegen?**

Buying Food

This lettuce is rather limp.	**Dieser Kopfsalat ist etwas welk.**
Are these apples crisp?	**Sind diese Äpfel frisch?**
I will put it in my carrier.	**Ich tue es in meine Tasche.**
Have you got a box?	**Haben Sie einen Karton?**

Vocabulary

apples	**die Äpfel**
apricots	**die Aprikosen**
asparagus	**der Spargel**
artichoke	**die Artischoke**
banana	**die Banane**
beans, broad	**die grossen Bohnen**
French	**die grünen Bohnen**
runner	**die Brechbohnen**
beetroot	**die Rote Beete**
broccoli	**Spargelkohl**
blackberry	**die Brombeere**
cabbage	**der Kohl**
carrots	**die Karotten**
cauliflower	**der Blumenkohl**
chestnut	**die Kastanie**
cherry	**die Kirsche**
cress	**die Kresse**
cucumber	**die Gurke**
date	**die Dattel**
fig	**die Feige**
grapefruit	**die Pampelmuse**
grapes	**die Weintrauben**
greengages	**die Reineclauden**
hazelnuts	**die Haselnüsse**
leeks	**der Porree**
lemon	**die Zitrone**

lettuce	der Kopfsalat
melon	die Melone
onions	die Zwiebeln
oranges	die Apfelsinen/Orangen
peaches	die Pfirsiche
pears	die Birnen
peas	die Erbsen
pineapple	die Ananas
plums	die Pflaumen
potatoes	die Kartoffeln
radishes	die Radieschen
raspberries	die Himbeeren
rhubarb	der Rhabarber
strawberries	die Erdbeeren
sweet corn	der Mais
sweet pepper	die Paprikaschoten
tangerines	die Mandarinen
tomatoes	die Tomaten
turnips	die weissen Rüben

At the grocer's/supermarket

bacon	der Speck
biscuits	das Kleingebäck/die Kekse
bottle (of)	eine Flasche
bread	das Brot
brush	die Bürste
butter	die Butter
cereals	die Cereals
cleaning fluid	das Reinigungsmittel
crisps	die Kartoffelchips
detergent	das Abwaschmittel
disinfectant	das Desinfektionsmittel
dried fruit	das Trockenobst
duster	das Staubtuch
eggs	die Eier
flour	das Mehl
jam	die Marmelade

jar (of)	**ein Glas**
margarine	**die Margarine**
oil	**das Öl**
paper napkins	**die Papierservietten**
rice	**der Reis**
salt	**das Salz**
tin (of)	**eine Dose**
vinegar	**der Essig**
washing powder	**das Waschpulver**

Other Shops

German towns and villages are full of shops run by individual shopkeepers. This makes shopping a pleasure for its variety as well as for the unique character of each establishment. Most shops are open from 8.30 to 1800 hours and even later in the summer. On Saturdays shops close in the afternoon.

I want to go shopping. Where are the best shops?	**Ich möchte einkaufen gehen. Wo sind die besten Geschäfte?**
the most popular shops?	**die beliebtesten Geschäfte?**
the cheaper shops?	**die billigeren Geschäfte?**
Where is the market?	**Wo ist der Markt?**
Till what time are you open?	**Bis wann sind Sie offen?**
Is there a grocer near here?	**Gibt es ein Lebensmittelgeschäft in der Nähe?**

VOCABULARY

antique shop	**der Antiquitätenladen**
art gallery	**die Kunstgalerie**
baker's shop	**die Bäckerei**
beauty salon	**der Kosmetiksalon**
bookshop	**die Buchhandlung**
butcher's shop	**der Fleischerladen/die Metzgerei**
chemist's shop	**die Drogerie**
dispensing chemist's shop	**die Apotheke**
confectionery	**das Süsswarengeschäft**
dairy	**die Molkerei**
delicatessen	**das Esswarengeschäft**
department store	**das Warenhaus**

87

Shopping

dry cleaner	die chemische Reinigung
fishmonger's shop	das Fischgeschäft
greengrocer's shop	das Gemüsegeschäft
grocer's shop	das Lebensmittelgeschäft
hairdresser	der Friseur
hardware store	das Eisenwarengeschäft
jeweller	der Juwelier
newsagent	der Zeitungshändler
off licence	die Spirituosenhandlung
optician	der Optiker
photographer's	das Photogeschäft
shoemaker	die Schuhmacherei
shoe shop	das Schuhgeschäft
stationer's shop	das Schreibwarengeschäft
tailor	der Herrenschneider
tobacconist's shop	das Tabakwarengeschäft
toy shop	das Spielwarengeschäft
travel agency	das Reisebüro
watchmaker	der Uhrmacher
wine merchant's shop	die Weinhandlung

Buying Clothes

I am just looking, thank you.	Ich möchte mich nur umsehen, vielen Dank.
I would like to look at some shirts.	Ich möchte mir gern ein paar Hemden ansehen.
plain shirts	einfarbige Hemden ansehen.
coloured shirts.	bunte Hemden ansehen.
striped shirts.	gestreifte Hemden ansehen.
cotton shirts.	Baumwoll hemden ansehen.
with long/short sleeves.	mit langen/kurzen Ärmeln.

My size is ...	**Meine Grösse ist ...**
My collar size is ...	**Meine Kragenweite ist ...**
This colour does not suit me.	**Diese Farbe steht mir nicht.**
It is not my style.	**Das ist nicht mein Stil.**
I want something more casual.	**Ich suche etwas Saloppes.**
Is there a fitting room where I can try it on?	**Haben Sie eine Umkleidekabine, wo ich es anprobieren kann?**
Can I return it if it is unsuitable?	**Kann ich es zurückbringen, wenn es nicht das Richtige ist?**
May I have a receipt?	**Könnte ich bitte eine Quittung haben?**
It does not fit. It is too large/small/narrow/wide.	**Es passt nicht. Es ist zu gross/klein/eng/weit.**
Can you show me something else?	**Könnten Sie mir etwas anderes zeigen?**

VOCABULARY

MATERIALS

camel hair	**das Kamelhaar**
chiffon	**der Chiffon**
cotton	**die Baumwolle**
crepe	**der Krepp**
denim	**der Denim**
felt	**der Filz**
flannel	**der Flanell**
gabardine	**der Gabardine**
lace	**die Spitze**

leather	das Leder
linen	das Leinen
nylon	das Nylon
piqué	der Pikee
poplin	der Poplin
rayon	das Rayon
satin	der Satin
silk	die Seide
suede	das Wildleder
taffeta	der Taft
tweed	der Tweed
velour	der Velours
velvet	der Samt
wool	die Wolle
worsted	das Kammgarn

MEASUREMENTS

arm	der Arm
leg	das Bein
chest	die Brust
waist	die Taille
neck	der Hals
hip	die Hüfte

COLOURS

biscuit	hellbraun
black	schwarz
blue	blau
green	grün
mauve	lila
orange	orangefarben
pastel colours	pastellfarben
red	rot
rose	rosa
strong colours	kräftige Farben
violet	violett

white	**weiss**
yellow	**gelb**

ITEMS OF CLOTHING

anorak	**der Anorak**
bathing hat	**die Badekappe**
bathrobe	**der Bademantel**
blazer	**der Blazer**
blouse	**die Bluse**
boots	**die Stiefel**
bra	**der Büstenhalter**
briefs	**die kurze Unterhose/die Shorts**
cap	**die Mütze**
cardigan	**die Strickjacke**
coat	**der Mantel**
dinner jacket	**der Smoking**
dress	**das Kleid**
girdle	**der Hüfthalter**
gloves	**die Handschuhe**
gym shoes	**die Turnschuhe**
handkerchief	**das Taschentuch**
hat	**der Hut**
jacket	**das Jackett**
jeans	**die Jeans**
jumper	**der Pullover/der Damenpulli**
negligé	**das Negligé**
nightdress	**das Nachthemd**
panties	**der Schlüpfer**
pant suit	**der Hosenanzug**
pullover	**der Pullover**
pyjamas	**der Schlafanzug**
raincoat	**der Regenmantel**
sandals	**die Sandalen**
scarf	**der Schal**
shirt	**das Hemd**
shoes	**die Schuhe**

Shopping

shorts	die Shorts
skirt	der Rock
slip	das Unterkleid
slippers	die Hausschuhe
stockings	die Strümpfe
suit	das Kostüm
suspenders	der Strumpfgürtel
swimsuit	der Badeanzug
T-shirt	das T-shirt
tie	die Krawatte
tights	die Strumpfhose
trousers	die Hose
press stud	der Druckknopf
hook and eyes	Haken und Ösen
twinset	der Twinset
underpants	die Unterhose
vest	das Unterhemd
waistcoat	die Weste
overcoat	der Mantel
belt	der Gürtel
buckle	die Schnalle
button	der Knopf
shoelaces	die Schnürsenkel
pocket	die Tasche
zip	der Reissverschluss
elastic	das Gummiband
thread	der Faden

At the Shoe Shop

I want a pair of walking shoes.	Ich möchte ein Paar Wanderschuhe/feste Schuhe.
evening shoes.	Abendschuhe.
moccasins.	Mokassins.
boots.	Stiefel.
suede shoes.	Wildlederschuhe.

slippers.	**Hausschuhe.**
sandals.	**Sandalen.**
canvas shoes.	**Segelschuhe.**

My size is ...   **Meine Grösse ist ...**

I like a broad/narrow fitting.   **Ich möchte einen weiten/ engen Schuh.**

high heels.	**hohe Absätze**
low/flat heels.	**niedrige/flache Absätze.**
shoes with leather soles.	**Schuhe mit Ledersohlen.**
shoes with rubber soles.	**Schuhe mit Gummisohlen.**
shoes with cork soles.	**Schuhe mit Korksohlen.**

These are not comfortable.   **Sie sind nicht bequem.**

May I try the other shoe?   **Könnte ich den anderen Schuh anprobieren?**

Have you got a shoe horn?   **Haben Sie einen Schuhanzieher?**

They are not my style.   **Die sind nicht, was ich suche.**

What other colours have you got?   **Welche anderen Farben haben Sie?**

How much are they?   **Wieviel kosten sie?**

That is more than I want to pay.   **Das ist mehr als ich ausgeben möchte.**

I will wear them. Will you please wrap up my old shoes?   **Ich möchte sie anbehalten. Würden Sie bitte meine alten Schuhe einpacken?**

Do you sell shoe polish/shoe cleaner/shoe brushes?   **Haben Sie Schuhkrem/ein Schuhreinigungsmittel/ Schuhbürsten?**

Shopping

Tobacconist's

Do you sell English cigarettes?	**Verkaufen Sie englische Zigaretten?**
Is that Virginian or French/Egyptian/Turkish/American tobacco?	**Ist das Virginiatabak oder französischer/aegyptischer/türkischer/amerikanischer Tabak?**
Have you any filter tip/king-size/menthol-cooled cigarettes?	**Haben Sie Filterzigaretten/extra-lange/Mentholzigaretten?**
Do you sell pipe tobacco?	**Haben Sie Pfeifentabak?**
May I see your selection of pipes?	**Könnte ich Ihr Pfeifensortiment sehen, bitte?**
I'd like a cigar.	**Ich möchte eine Zigarre.**
A packet/carton of cigarettes, please.	**Eine Schachtel/eine Packung Zigaretten, bitte.**
A box of matches, please.	**Eine Schachtel Streichhölzer, bitte.**
Have you a cigar cutter?	**Haben Sie einen Zigarrenabschneider?**
Do you sell pipe cleaners?	**Haben Sie Pfeifenreiniger?**
I'd like some snuff.	**Ich möchte Schnupftabak.**

VOCABULARY

carton	**der Karton/die Packung**
case	**das Etui**
cigarette lighter	**das Feuerzeug**
flint	**der Feuerstein**

94

gas	das Feuerzeuggas
lighter fluid	das Feuerzeugbenzin
matches	die Streichhölzer
packet	die Schachtel
pipe	die Pfeife
pipe-cleaner	der Pfeifenreiniger
pouch	der Beutel

Hardware Stores and Electrical Goods

I'd like a heavy-duty saucepan/frying pan.	Ich möchte einen stabilen Kochtopf/eine Bratpfanne.
Have you a grill/charcoal?	Haben Sie einen Grill/Holzkohle?
I need a plastic/metal can for water.	Ich brauche eine Plastik-Wasserkanne/eine Wasserkanne aus Metall.
I'd like a bucket.	Ich möchte einen Eimer.
Give me a ball of strong twine, please.	Geben Sie mir bitte ein Knäuel starken Bindfaden.
I need a tow rope and a hook.	Ich brauche ein Schlepptau und einen Haken.

VOCABULARY

adaptor	der Zwischenstecker
basket	der Korb
battery	die Batterie
brush	die Bürste
bulb	die Birne
car radio	das Autoradio
chamois leather	das Fensterleder

Shopping

distilled water	**das destillierte Wasser**
fork	**die Gabel**
hammer	**der Hammer**
insulating tape	**das Isolierband**
knife	**das Messer**
mallet	**der Holzhammer**
penknife	**das Taschenmesser**
percolator	**die Kaffeemaschine**
saw	**die Säge**
scissors	**die Schere**
screwdriver	**der Schraubenzieher**
shaver	**der elektrische Rasierapparat**
spoon	**der Löffel**
string	**der Bindfaden**
tweezers	**die Pinzette**
wrench	**der Schraubenschlüssel**
wire	**der Draht**

Chemist

In Germany there are two kinds of chemist. An **Apotheke** is a dispensing chemist's or pharmacy. A **Drogerie** sells the kind of goods generally available in chemists' shops.

Do I need a doctor's prescription?	**Brauche ich ein ärztliches Rezept?**
Is there an all-night chemist open?	**Gibt es eine Apotheke mit Nachtdienst?**
Can you make up this prescription?	**Können Sie mir dieses Rezept machen?**
When will it be ready?	**Wann ist es fertig?**

Will you write down the instructions? In English if possible.	**Würden Sie bitte die Anweisung aufschreiben? Wenn möglich auf Englisch.**
Is this all right/dangerous for children?	**Ist dies harmlos/gefährlich für Kinder?**
Have you anything for a cold/ sore throat/cough?	**Haben Sie ein Mittel gegen Erkältung/Halsschmerzen/ Husten?**
I'd like to buy a thermometer.	**Ich möchte ein Fieber- thermometer kaufen.**
Would you please have a look at this cut/bruise?	**Würden Sie sich bitte diese Schnittwunde/diese Schramme ansehen?**
What kind of bandage would be best?	**Was für ein Verband ist am besten?**
I've got indigestion.	**Ich habe Verdauungsstörungen.**
diarrhoea.	**Durchfall.**
constipation.	**Verstopfung.**
a headache.	**Kopfschmerzen.**
an upset stomach.	**eine Magenverstimmung.**
sunburn.	**einen Sonnenbrand.**

VOCABULARY

MEDICINES

aspirin	**Aspirin**
antibiotic	**Antibiotika**
bandage	**der Verband**
band-aids	**das Heftpflaster**
contraceptive	**das Verhütungsmittel**

corn plaster	**das Hühneraugenpflaster**
cotton wool	**die Watte**
cough mixture	**der Hustensaft**
cough lozenges	**die Hustenpastillen**
disinfectant	**das Desinfektionsmittel**
ear drops	**die Ohrentropfen**
gargle	**das Gurgelwasser**
gauze	**der Verbandmull**
insect repellant	**das Insektenmittel**
iodine	**das Jod**
iron pills	**die Eisentabletten**
laxative	**das Abführmittel**
lip salve	**die Lippensalbe**
sanitary towels	**die Damenbinde**
sedative	**das Beruhigungsmittel**
sleeping pills	**die Schlaftabletten**
tranquillizers	**das Beruhigungsmittel**
thermometer	**das Fieberthermometer**
vitamins	**die Vitamintabletten**

TOILET ARTICLES

after shave	**das Rasierwasser**
astringent	**das Adstringens**
bath salts	**das Badesalz**
bath oil	**das Badeöl**
cologne	**das Kölnischwasser**
cream	**die Creme**
cleansing	**die Reinigungscreme**
cuticle	**die Nagelhautcreme**
foundation	**die Make-up Unterlage**
moisturising	**die Feuchtigkeitscreme**
deodorant	**das Desodorans**
emery board	**die Sandpapierfeile**
eyebrow pencil	**der Augenbrauenstift**
eye shadow	**der Lidschatten**
face pack	**die Gesichtsmaske**

face powder	**der Gesichtspuder**
lipstick	**der Lippenstift**
nailbrush	**die Nagelbürste**
nailfile	**die Nagelfeile**
nail polish	**der Nagellack**
nail polish remover	**der Nagellackentferner**
perfume	**das Parfüm**
rouge	**das Rouge**
safety pins	**die Sicherheitsnadeln**
shampoo	**das Shampoo**
shaving brush	**der Rasierpinsel**
shaving cream	**die Rasiercreme**
soap	**die Seife**
sponge	**der Schwamm**
suntan oil	**das Sonnenöl**
tissues	**die Papiertücher**
toilet paper	**das Toilettenpapier**
toothbrush	**die Zahnbürste**
toothpaste	**die Zahnpasta**

At the Photographer's

I'd like to buy a camera.	**Ich möchte eine Kamera kaufen.**
I'd like a camera that is cheap and easy to use.	**Ich möchte eine billige und einfache Kamera.**
Will you please check my camera?	**Würden Sie bitte meine Kamera prüfen?**
The film is sticking.	**Der Film klemmt.**
The exposure meter is not working.	**Das Bildzählwerk funktioniert nicht.**
The flash does not light up.	**Das Blitzlicht funktioniert nicht.**

Shopping

The film winder is jammed.	**Der Filmtransport klemmt.**
Can you do it soon?	**Können Sie es bald machen?**
Will you please process this film?	**Würden Sie bitte diesen Film entwickeln?**
I want some black and white/colour film.	**Ich möchte ein paar Schwarzweissfilme/Farbfilme.**
Is this film for use in daylight or artificial light?	**Ist dies ein Tageslichtfilm oder ein Kunstlichtfilm?**
I need a light meter.	**Ich brauche einen Lichtmesser.**
How much is an electronic flash?	**Wie teuer ist ein elektronisches Blitzlicht?**

VOCABULARY

Films 120, 127, 135	**Filme einhundertzwanzig, einhundertsiebenundzwanzig, einhundertfünfunddreissig**
20 exposures, 36 exposures	**zwanzig Aufnahmen, sechsunddreissig Aufnahmen**
a fast film	**ein hochempfindlicher Film Film**
a fine-grain film	**ein Feinkornfilm**
cinefilm 8mm/16mm	**ein Cinefilm acht Millimeter/sechzehn Millimeter**
flash bulbs	**Blitzlampen**
lens	**das Objektiv**
red filter	**der Rotfilter**
yellow filter	**der Gelbfilter**
ultra-violet filter	**der Ultraviolettfilter**
range finder	**der Entfernungsmesser**

100

shutter	**der Verschluss**
reflex camera	**die Spiegelreflex Kamera**
long-focus lens	**das Teleobjektiv**
wide-angle lens	**das Weitwinkelobjektiv**

Bookshop/Stationer's

Where can I find the books on art/history/politics/sport?	**Wo finde ich Bücher über Kunst/Geschichte/Politik/Sport?**
Where can I find the guide books?	**Wo finde ich Reiseführer?**
Have you any English newspapers?	**Führen Sie englische Zeitungen?**
Have you any English paperbacks?	**Haben Sie englische Taschenbücher**
Can you recommend an easy book to read in German?	**Können Sie mir ein leichtes Buch in Deutsch empfehlen?**
Do you sell second-hand books?	**Verkaufen Sie alte Bücher?**
I want a map of the area.	**Ich möchte eine Karte von dieser Gegend.**
The scale of this map is too small.	**Der Masstab dieser Karte ist zu klein.**
Have you got refills for this ballpoint pen?	**Haben Sie Ersatzminen für diesen Kugelschreiber?**
Can you please deliver the English newspaper every morning?	**Könnten Sie bitte die englische Zeitung jeden Morgen ins Haus liefern?**

VOCABULARY

address book	das Adressbuch
box of crayons	die Schachtel Buntstifte
carbon paper	das Durchschlagpapier
cellophane	das Zellophan
drawing paper	das Zeichenpapier
drawing pins	die Reisszwecken
envelopes	die Briefumschläge
exercise book	das Schreibheft
fountain pen	der Füller
greaseproof paper	das Pergamentpapier
glue	der Klebstoff
ink	die Tinte
label	das Etikett
notebook	das Notizbuch
notepaper	das Briefpapier
paste	der Leim
pen	die Feder
pencil	der Bleistift
pencil sharpener	der Bleistiftspitzer
playing cards	die Spielkarten
rubber	der Radiergummi
ruler	das Lineal
silver foil	die Aluminiumfolie
typewriter ribbon	das Farbband
typing paper	das Schreibmaschinenpapier
writing pad	der Schreibblock

Buying Souvenirs

Are all these things made in
Germany?

Sind alle diese Artikel
deutsche Fabrikate?

I like this bag.	**Diese Tasche gefällt mir.**
Have you any costume jewellery?	**Haben Sie Modeschmuck?**
I'm looking for bracelet charms.	**Ich möchte Armbandamulette.**
I'd like to try on that ring.	**Ich möchte den Ring anprobieren.**
What is this bracelet made of?	**Woraus ist dieses Armband?**
I collect copperware. Have you any pots?	**Ich sammle Kupfersachen. Haben Sie Kupferbehälter?**
I'd like some local pottery.	**Ich möchte hiesige Keramik.**
Can you pack this carefully?	**Könnten Sie dies bitte sorgfältig einpacken?**
Do you despatch things abroad?	**Versenden Sie Waren ins Ausland?**
I'm just looking around.	**Ich möchte mich nur umsehen.**
I will come back later.	**Ich werde wiederkommen.**
Can I leave a deposit on it and return tomorrow?	**Könnte ich eine Anzahlung machen und morgen wiederkommen?**
Do you take foreign cheques with a Eurocard?	**Nehmen Sie ausländische Schecks mit Eurokarte an?**

VOCABULARY

beads	**die Perlen**
brooch	**die Brosche**

Shopping

chain	die Kette
cigarette lighter	das Feuerzeug
clock	die Uhr
cuff links	die Manschettenknöpfe
earrings	die Ohrringe
jewel box	der Schmuckkasten
music box	die Spieldose
necklace	die Halskette
rosary	der Rosenkranz
silverware	das Tafelsilber
watchstrap	das Uhrenarmband
wristwatch	die Armbanduhr

Entertainment

Out for the Evening

Nightclubs

Can you recommend a nightclub with a good show?	**Können Sie einen Nachtklub mit einem guten Programm empfehlen?**
a place with dancing and cabaret?	**ein Lokal mit Tanz und Kabarett empfehlen?**
a disco?	**eine Diskothek empfehlen?**
an open-air dance?	**Tanzen im Freien empfehlen?**
a nightclub with hostesses?	**einen Nachtklub mit Hostessen empfehlen?**
Is there an entrance fee?	**Muss man Eintritt bezahlen?**
Does it include drinks?	**Sind die Getränke einbegriffen?**
What is the cost of drinks?	**Wie teuer sind die Getränke?**
At what time does the show start?	**Wann fängt das Programm an?**
Is there a different price for drinks at the bar?	**Bezahlt man andere Preise für Getränke an der Bar?**
I do not want a photograph.	**Ich möchte kein Foto.**
May I have this dance?	**Darf ich zum Tanz bitten?**

Theatre/Opera

Is there a ticket agency near?	**Gibt es eine Theaterkartenagentur in der Nähe?**

Entertainment

How can I get a ticket?	**Wie könnte ich eine Karte bekommen?**
Are there any last-minute returns?	**Kann man zurückgegebene Karten kurz vor der Vorstellung bekommen?**
Do we have to wear evening dress?	**Muss man Abendgarderobe tragen?**
I'd like a souvenir programme.	**Ich möchte ein Programmheft bitte.**
What is the name of the prima donna?	**Wie heisst die Primadonna?**
Who is the leading actor?	**Wer ist der Hauptdarsteller?**

VOCABULARY

applause	**der Beifall**
audience	**das Publikum**
bass	**der Bass**
baritone	**der Bariton**
composer	**der Komponist**
conductor	**der Dirigent**
contralto	**der Alt**
encore	**das Encore**
orchestra	**das Orchester**
playwright	**der Bühnenautor**
scenery	**die Bühnenausstattung**
soprano	**der Sopran**
stage	**die Bühne**
tenor	**der Tenor**

Cinema

What is on at the cinema?	**Was läuft im Kino?**
Have you got a guide to what's on?	**Haben Sie einen Veranstaltungskalender?**
Two stalls/circle seats, please.	**Zwei Plätze im Parkett/Ersten Rang, bitte.**
Will we have to queue for long?	**Muss man lange anstehen?**
I want a seat near the front/at the back/in the middle.	**Ich möchte einen Platz vorne/hinten/in der Mitte haben.**
I'd rather sit over there.	**Ich sitze lieber da drüben.**
Will you please shine your torch here?	**Würden Sie bitte mit Ihrer Taschenlampe hierherleuchten?**
I have dropped something.	**Ich habe etwas fallenlassen.**
Is there an ice cream seller?	**Wird hier Eiskrem verkauft?**
At what time does the main film start?	**Wann fängt der Hauptfilm an?**
Will you please move over to the right/left.	**Würden Sie bitte etwas nach rechts/links rücken.**
Please will you remove your hat.	**Bitte, nehmen Sie Ihren Hut ab.**

VOCABULARY

actor	**der Schauspieler**
actress	**die Schauspielerin**
director	**der Filmregisseur**
dubbing	**das Synchronisieren**

Entertainment

interval	die Pause
producer	der Produzent
projector	der Projektor
screen	die Leinwand
sound	der Ton
star	der Star

Concert Hall

I want a seat from which I can see the pianist's hands.	Ich möchte einen Platz, von dem ich die Hände des Pianisten sehen kann.
Can I buy the score?	Kann man die Partitur kaufen?
Who is conducting tonight?	Wer dirigiert heute abend?
Who is the soloist?	Wer ist der Solist?

VOCABULARY

bassoon	das Fagott
brass	die Blechbläser
cello	das Cello
clarinet	die Klarinette
cymbal	die Zimbel
double bass	die Bassgeige
drum	die Trommel
flute	die Flöte
French horn	das Horn
percussion	das Schlagzeug
saxophone	das Saxophon
strings	die Saiteninstrumente
timpani	die Kesselpauke
trombone	die Posaune

trumpet	**die Trompete**
violin	**die Violine**
wind instrument	**das Blasinstrument**

Casino

What games are played here?	**Was wird hier gespielt?**
What is the minimum stake in this room?	**Was ist der niedrigste Einsatz in diesem Raum?**
Can I buy some chips?	**Kann ich Spielmarken kaufen?**
I should like 100 Marks' worth.	**Für hundert Mark, bitte.**
Excuse me, those are my chips.	**Verzeihung, das sind meine Spielmarken.**
Where can I cash my chips?	**Wo kann ich meine Spielmarken einlösen?**
I'm bust.	**Ich habe kein Geld mehr.**
I'll take another card.	**Ich nehme noch eine Karte.**
No more.	**Nein danke.**
Pass me the dice, please.	**Reichen Sie mir bitte die Würfel.**

VOCABULARY

ace	**das As**
bet	**die Wette**
cards	**die Karten**
chemin de fer	**Chemin de Fer**
clubs	**Kreuz**

craps	**Craps**
croupier	**der Croupier**
diamonds	**Karo**
evens	**gleich**
hearts	**Herz**
jack	**der Bube**
joker	**der Joker**
king	**der König**
poker	**Poker**
pontoon	**das Vingt-et-un**
queen	**die Dame**
shoe	**der Schuh**
spades	**Pik**

Out for the Day

On the Beach

Does one have to pay to use this beach?	**Muss man an diesem Strand bezahlen?**
Is there a free section of the beach?	**Gibt es einen freien Strand?**
Is it clean?	**Ist er sauber?**
How much does it cost per day/per week to hire a cabin?	**Wie teuer ist es, pro Tag/pro Woche, eine Kabine zu mieten?**
a beach chair?	**einen Strandkorb zu mieten?**
a deckchair?	**einen Liegestuhl zu mieten?**
an air mattress?	**eine Luftmatratze zu mieten?**
a sun umbrella?	**einen Sonnenschirm zu mieten?**
Can I leave valuables in the cabin?	**Kann man Wertgegenstände in der Kabine lassen?**
Is the ticket valid all day?	**Ist die Karte den ganzen Tag gültig?**
Does the beach shelve steeply?	**Wird das Wasser schnell tief?**
Is it safe for swimming?	**Kann man hier ohne Gefahr schwimmen?**
Are there any currents?	**Gibt es hier Strömungen?**
Is it safe to dive off the rocks?	**Ist es gefährlich, von den Felsen ins Wasser zu springen?**

On the Beach

Where are the showers?	**Wo sind die Duschen?**
Have you any tar remover?	**Haben Sie Teerentferner?**
Can I hire a swimsuit/trunks?	**Kann ich einen Badeanzug/ Badehosen mieten?**
I've cut my foot. Have you any elastoplast?	**Ich habe meinen Fuss verletzt. Haben Sie Heftpflaster?**
Is there a lost property office?	**Gibt es hier ein Fundbüro?**
Is there a children's beach club?	**Gibt es hier einen Strandklub für Kinder?**
At what time are the keep fit classes?	**Wann findet die Gymnastikstunde statt?**
Is there water ski tuition available?	**Kann man Unterricht in Wasserschi bekommen?**
Does it matter if I can't swim?	**Ich kann nicht schwimmen. Macht das etwas?**
Where is the nearest beach shop?	**Wo ist das nächste Strandartikelgeschäft?**
Have you got a life jacket?	**Haben Sie eine Schwimmweste?**
Is this a good place for skin diving?	**Ist dies eine gute Stelle zum Sporttauchen?**
Help! I'm in difficulty.	**Hilfe! Ich bin in Not.**

VOCABULARY

beach ball	**der Wasserball**
goggles	**die Schutzbrille**
harpoon gun	**die Harpune**
high tide	**Flut**

lilo	die Luftmatratze
low tide	die Ebbe
net	das Netz
promenade	die Promenade
pedalo	das Pedalo
pines	die Kiefern
raft	das Floss
rocks	die Felsen
rowing boat	das Ruderboot
sand	der Sand
sandals	die Sandalen
sea	die See
seaweed	der Seetang
shells	die Muscheln
shingle	der Strandkiesel
sun oil	das Sonnenöl
surf	die Brandung
surf board	das Gleitbrett
underwater	Unterwasser
waterski instructor	der Wasserschilehrer
yacht	die Jacht

Sightseeing

Where can I get a good guide book?	Wo kann ich einen guten Reiseführer bekommen?
Is there an excursion round the city?	Gibt es eine Stadtrundfahrt?
Is it a conducted party?	Ist es eine Gruppe mit Fremdenführer?
Am I allowed to go round alone?	Ist es erlaubt, allein umherzugehen?
Where do I find an official guide?	Wo finde ich einen Fremdenführer?

Sightseeing

Does the whole-day excursion include lunch?	**Ist Mittagessen im Ganztagsausflug einbegriffen?**
Are the entrance fees extra?	**Sind die Eintrittsgebühren extra?**
Should I tip the guide/driver?	**Gibt man dem Fremdenführer/dem Fahrer ein Trinkgeld?**
I'd like to stay here longer.	**Ich möchte hier etwas länger bleiben.**
I'll meet the party later.	**Ich schliesse mich der Gruppe später wieder an.**
Where will you be?	**Wo werden Sie sein?**
Will you please write it down?	**Würden Sie es bitte aufschreiben?**
Can I hire an audioguide?	**Kann ich einen Audioapparat mieten?**

In Churches

Do ladies have to cover their heads?	**Müssen Damen eine Kopfbedeckung tragen?**
Is it all right to enter like this?	**Darf man so die Kirche betreten?**
How old is this church?	**Wie alt ist diese Kirche?**
Who founded it?	**Wer hat sie gegründet?**
Are the stained glass windows original?	**Sind das die Originalbuntglasfenster?**
Can one illuminate the fresco?	**Kann das Freskogemälde beleuchtet werden?**

114

Is one allowed to go up to the bell tower?	**Darf man den Glockenturm besteigen?**
Is there a book about the church?	**Gibt es ein Buch über die Kirche?**
May I leave a small contribution?	**Darf ich eine kleine Geldspende machen?**

VOCABULARY

abbey	**die Abtei**
aisles	**die Seitenschiffe**
altar	**der Altar**
arch	**der Bogen**
basilica	**die Basilika**
candle	**die Kerze**
cathedral	**die Kathedrale/der Dom**
chapel	**die Kapelle**
choir	**der Chor**
cloister	**der Kreuzgang**
column	**die Säule**
convent	**der Konvent**
crucifix	**das Kruzifix**
crypt	**die Gruft**
font	**das Taufbecken**
fresco	**das Fresko**
monastery	**das Kloster**
nave	**das Kirchenschiff**
rood	**das Kruzifix**
sculpture	**die Skulptur**
shrine	**der Schrein**
west front	**die westliche Fassade**

Sightseeing

Art Galleries and Museums

Have you a catalogue?	**Haben Sie einen Katalog?**
Have you an illustrated catalogue?	**Haben Sie einen illustrierten Katalog?**
Are there any plaster casts?	**Haben Sie Gipsabdrücke?**
Do you sell transparencies?	**Verkaufen Sie Diapositive?**
Am I allowed to take photographs?	**Darf ich hier fotografieren?**
May I use my tripod?	**Darf ich mein Stativ aufstellen?**
Is the gallery open on Sundays?	**Ist die Galerie sonntags geöffnet?**
Is it free?	**Ist der Eintritt frei?**
Where can I find the Dutch School?	**Wo finde ich die holländische Schule?**
Do you make photocopies?	**Machen Sie Fotokopien?**
Where is the library?	**Wo ist die Bibliothek?**

VOCABULARY

antique books	**antiquarische Bücher**
bas relief	**das Bas-Relief**
china	**das Porzellan**
costumes	**die Kostüme**
drawing	**die Zeichnung**
engraving	**der Holzschnitt**
etching	**der Kupferstich**
frame	**der Rahmen**
furniture	**die Möbel**

jewellery	der Schmuck
lithograph	die Lithographie
miniature	die Miniatur
porcelain	das Porzellan
pottery	die Töpferware
silverware	das Tafelsilber

Historical Sights

Is it far to walk?	Ist es weit zu gehen?
Can I wait here till you return?	Könnte ich hier warten, bis Sie zurückkommen?
Is there a souvenir stall?	Gibt es einen Andenkenladen?
Where can we get a cold drink?	Wo können wir ein kaltes Getränk bekommen?
Is there a plan of the grounds?	Gibt es einen Plan der ganzen Anlage?
I would like to walk round the gardens.	Ich möchte durch die Grünanlagen gehen.

Vocabulary

arena	die Arena
aqueduct	der Aquaedukt
amphitheatre	das Amphitheater
armour	die Rüstung
battlements	die Zinnen
catacombs	die Katakomben
cannon	die Kanone
castle	das Schloss
courtyard	der Hof

Sightseeing

crossbow	die Armbrust
fort	das Fort
fortifications	die Befestigungen
forum	das Forum
fountain	der Springbrunnen
gate	das Tor
pediment	der Giebel
portcullis	das Fallgatter
viaduct	der Viadukt
wall	die Mauer

Gardens

Are these gardens open to the public?	Sind diese Anlagen fürs Publikum geöffnet?
Can we walk where we like?	Dürfen wir überall herumgehen?
How long will it take to walk around?	Wie lange dauert es, ganz durchzugehen?
At what time do you close?	Wann schliessen Sie?
Is there a plan of the gardens?	Gibt es einen Plan der Anlagen?
Where is the greenhouse/tropical plant house?	Wo ist das Gewächshaus/das Haus mit den tropischen Pflanzen?
May we sit on the grass?	Dürfen wir auf dem Gras sitzen?
What is the name of that plant/flower?	Wie heisst diese Pflanze/Blume?
Is there a lake/a pond?	Gibt es einen See/einen Teich?

Who designed these gardens?	**Wer hat diese Anlagen entworfen?**

VOCABULARY

ash	die Esche
beech	die Buche
birch	die Birke
bougainvillea	die Bougainvillea
carnation	die Nelke
cherry	der Kirschbaum
chrysanthemum	die Chrysantheme
clematis	die Klematis
daffodil	die Narzisse
dahlia	die Dahlie
daisy	das Gänseblümchen
deciduous trees	Laubbäume
elm	die Ulme
evergreen	das Immergrün
fir	die Tanne
geranium	die Geranie
herbaceous border	die Blumenrabatte
ivy	der Efeu
lily	die Lilie
moss	das Moos
nasturtium	die Kapuzinerkresse
oak	die Eiche
pear	der Birnbaum
pine	die Kiefer
plane	die Platane
poplar	die Pappel
rose	die Rose
tulip	die Tulpe
violet	das Veilchen
wisteria	die Wisterie

Sightseeing

The Zoo

The children would like to visit the zoo.	**Die Kinder möchten den Zoo besuchen.**
Is it open every day?	**Ist er jeden Tag offen?**
Is there a nature reserve?	**Gibt es da ein Naturschutzgebiet?**
Can one drive through it?	**Kann man da durchfahren?**
Where can we park the car?	**Wo können wir parken?**
Where can one buy animal food?	**Wo können wir Tierfutter kaufen?**
When is feeding time?	**Wann sind die Fütterungszeiten?**
Is there an insect house?	**Gibt es hier ein Insektenhaus?**
Is there a childrens' zoo?	**Gibt es einen Kinderzoo?**

VOCABULARY

aquarium	**das Aquarium**
ants	**die Ameisen**
antelope	**die Antilope**
baboon	**der Pavian**
bat	**die Fledermaus**
bison	**der Bison**
bird	**der Vogel**
cat	**die Katze**
crocodile	**das Krokodil**
dog	**der Hund**
frog	**der Frosch**
giraffe	**die Giraffe**
hippopotamus	**das Nilpferd**

horse	**das Pferd**
hyena	**die Hyäne**
lion	**der Löwe**
leopard	**der Leopard**
parrot	**der Papagei**
rhinoceros	**das Rhinozeros**
seal	**der Seehund**
snake	**die Schlange**
turtle	**die Schildkröte**
zebra	**das Zebra**

Sport

The chief spectator sport in Germany is football. Germans are also keen supporters of motor racing, ice hockey, horse racing and sailing. In Bavaria there is good river and lake fishing, but you need a licence. In winter there is good skiing in the Bavarian Alps.

Football

Where is the stadium?	**Wo ist das Stadion?**
How does one get there?	**Wie kommt man dahin?**
Should I book tickets?	**Sollte ich Karten buchen?**
Will it be very crowded?	**Wird es da sehr voll sein?**
Who is playing?	**Wer spielt?**
Is there a local team?	**Gibt es eine Lokalmannschaft?**
I want a ticket for the main stand.	**Ich möchte eine Karte für die Haupttribüne.**
a place under cover/in the open.	**unterm Dach/im Freien.**
May I have a programme?	**Könnte ich ein Programm haben?**

VOCABULARY

attack	**der Angriff**
area	**der Bereich**
defence	**die Verteidigung**
goalkeeper	**der Torwart**
goal posts	**die Torpfosten**
halfway line	**die Mittellinie**

penalty area	**der Strafraum**
players	**die Spieler**
referee	**der Schiedsrichter**
team	**die Mannschaft**

Race Meetings

I want a ticket for the paddock/a grandstand seat, please.	**Ich möchte eine Karte für den Sattelplatz/einen Haupttribünenplatz bitte.**
Where can I place a bet?	**Wo kann ich meine Wette platzieren?**
What are the odds on number 5?	**Was sind die Gewinnchancen von Nummer fünf?**
I'd like to back it to win/each way/for a place.	**Ich möchte auf Sieg setzen/auf alle Plätze setzen/auf einen Platz setzen.**
Which is the favourite?	**Wer ist der Favorit?**
I will back the outsider.	**Ich möchte auf den Aussenseiter setzen.**
Is the jockey well known?	**Ist der Jockei bekannt?**

<small>VOCABULARY</small>

course	**die Rennbahn**
filly	**das Füllen**
flat	**das Flachrennen**
horse	**das Pferd**
hurdles	**die Hürden**
jockey	**der Jockei**
owner	**der Besitzer**
photo finish	**das Photofinish**

Sport

rails	das Geländer
stable	der Stall
starting gate	das Startgatter
tote	der Totalisator/das Toto
trainer	der Trainer

Tennis

Is there a tennis club near here?	**Gibt es einen Tennisklub in der Nähe?**
Where is the championship being held?	**Wo findet das Meisterschaftsspiel statt?**
How can I get some tickets?	**Wie kann ich Karten bekommen?**
Should I arrive early?	**Muss man früh da sein?**
Who is playing?	**Wer spielt?**
Is it on hard courts or grass?	**Spielt man auf Lehm oder Gras?**
I want to watch the men's singles/doubles/mixed doubles.	**Ich möchte das Herreneinzel sehen/das Doppel sehen/das gemischte Doppel sehen.**
How do you score in German?	**Wie zählen Sie Punkte auf Deutsch?**
15, 30, 40, deuce, advantage in/out, game, set, match.	**Fünfzehn, dreissig, vierzig, Einstand, Vorteil in/aus, Spiel, Satz, das Tennismatch.**
Shall we toss for service?	**Sollen wir für Service losen?**

Let's adjust the net.	**Lassen Sie uns das Netz in Ordnung bringen.**
It's too high/too low.	**Es ist zu hoch/zu niedrig.**
That was out/in/on the line.	**Das war aus/in/auf der Linie.**
Good shot.	**Das war ein guter Schlag.**
Will you keep the score?	**Würden Sie bitte zählen?**
Change ends.	**Seiten wechseln.**

Vocabulary

backhand	**Rückhand**
forehand	**Vorhand**
racquet	**der Tennisschläger**
rally	**der Ballwechsel**
smash	**der Schmetterball**
spin	**der Schleuderball**
tennis ball	**der Tennisball**
umpire	**der Schiedsrichter**
volley	**die Volley**

Golf

Is there a golf course near by?	**Gibt es einen Golfplatz in der Nähe?**
Does one have to be a member?	**Muss man Mitglied sein?**
Is there temporary membership?	**Gibt es eine provisorische Mitgliedschaft?**
How much does it cost to play?	**Wie teuer ist das Spielen?**
I'd like a caddy.	**Ich möchte einen Caddie.**

Are there any trolleys for hire?	**Kann man einen Karren mieten?**
I'd like to speak to the professional.	**Ich möchte den Profi sprechen.**
Could you give me a lesson?	**Können Sie mir eine Stunde geben?**
Will you play a round with me?	**Würden Sie eine Runde mit mir spielen?**
My handicap is eighteen.	**Mein Handikap ist achtzehn.**
My problem is a slice/a hook.	**Mein Problem ist ein Slice/ ein Hook.**
My drive is not long enough.	**Mein Treibschlag ist nicht lang genug.**
My approach shots are weak.	**Mein Annäherungsschlag ist schwach.**
I'll do some putting while I wait for you.	**Ich werde etwas putten, während ich auf Sie warte.**
Can I hire some clubs?	**Kann ich Golfschläger mieten?**
May I have a scorecard?	**Könnte ich eine Punktkarte haben?**

VOCABULARY

bunker	**der Bunker**
birdie	**das Birdie**
club house	**das Klubhaus**
eagle	**der Eagle**
fairway	**die Rasenfläche**
golf bag	**der Köcher**
green	**das Grün**

irons	die Eisen
mashie	der Mashie
niblick	der Niblick (Golfschläger)
par	par
rough	das Rough
tee	das Abschlagmal

Water Skiing

I have never skiied before.	Ich war noch nie auf Skiern.
I am not a good swimmer.	Ich bin kein guter Schwimmer.
Do I wear a life jacket?	Muss ich eine Schwimmweste tragen?
Will you please help me to put on the skis?	Würden Sie mir bitte in die Skier helfen?
Please pass me the rope.	Bitte reichen Sie mir das Seil.
May I ride on the speed boat?	Darf ich im Rennboot mitfahren?
Can I borrow a wetsuit?	Kann ich mir einen Taucheranzug leihen?
I'm ready now.	Ich bin jetzt fertig.
Just a moment.	Einen Augenblick, bitte.

VOCABULARY

| aquaplane | das Gleitbrett (zum Wellenreiten) |
| bathing hat | die Badekappe |

Sport

goggles	**die Schutzbrille**
jump	**der Sprung**
monoski	**der Einzelschi**
slalom	**der Slalom**

Riding

Is there a riding stable here?	**Gibt es hier einen Reitstall?**
Can I hire a horse for riding?	**Kann ich ein Reitpferd mieten?**
Do you give lessons?	**Geben Sie Reitstunden?**
I'd like to go on a hack.	**Ich möchte einen Ausritt machen.**
I'd like a quiet horse.	**Ich möchte ein ruhiges Pferd.**
Have you any ponies?	**Haben Sie Ponies?**
Will an instructor accompany the ride?	**Wird ein Reitlehrer den Ausritt begleiten?**
I'd like to practise jumping.	**Ich möchte das Springen üben.**
I am an experienced rider/a novice.	**Ich kann gut reiten/ich bin ein Anfänger.**
Do you have English saddles?	**Haben Sie englische Sattel?**
This horse has gone lame.	**Dieses Pferd ist lahm.**
The girth is too loose.	**Der Gurt ist zu lose.**
Will you please adjust my stirrups?	**Würden Sie bitte meine Steigbügel verstellen?**

Will you hold my horse while I get on?	**Würden Sie bitte das Pferd halten, während ich aufsteige.**
Will you give me a leg up?	**Würden Sie mir bitte hinaufhelfen?**

VOCABULARY

bit	**das Pferdegebiss**
bridle	**der Zaum**
harness	**der Harnisch**
hoof	**der Huf**
hock	**das Sprunggelenk**
martingale	**der Martingal**
mare	**die Stute**
reins	**die Zügel**
stallion	**der Hengst**
withers	**der Widerrist**

Fishing

Where can I get a permit to fish?	**Wo bekomme ich eine Angelerlaubnis?**
Are there places for fishing in this area?	**Gibt es in dieser Gegend Angelstellen?**
Are there any trout or salmon?	**Gibt es hier Forellen oder Lachs?**
How much does a day's fishing cost?	**Wie teuer ist das Angeln pro Tag?**
Is that per rod?	**Ist das pro Rute?**
Where can I get some bait?	**Wo kann ich Fischköder bekommen?**

Sport

Is there a minimum size that I am allowed to keep?	**Gibt es eine Minimumgrösse von Fisch, die ich behalten darf?**
What is the best time of day for fishing?	**Was ist die beste Tageszeit zum Fischen?**
Are there any boats that will take me deep-sea fishing?	**Gibt es Boote, die mich zum Hochseefischen mitnehmen?**
Do they provide tackle?	**Stellen sie die Geräte zur Verfügung?**

VOCABULARY

fishing season	**die Angelsaison**
fly	**die Fliege**
float	**der Schwimmer**
gaff	**der Fischhaken**
hook	**der Angelhaken**
line	**die Angelschnur**
lure	**der Fischköder**
net	**das Netz**
reel	**die Spule**
spinner	**der Spinner**
weights	**die Gewichte**

Shooting

Where can I shoot?	**Wo kann ich schiessen?**
Do I need a licence?	**Brauche ich eine Lizenz?**
I'd like to hire a 12-bore shotgun.	**Ich möchte eine zwölfkalibrige Schrotflinte mieten.**

I have my own rifle.	**Ich habe mein eigenes Gewehr.**
Is there a shooting party I could join?	**Gibt es eine Schiessgruppe, der ich beitreten kann?**
Is there a clay pigeon shoot?	**Gibt es einen Tontaubenschiesstand?**
Is there a rifle range near?	**Gibt es einen Schiesstand in der Nähe?**
When does the season for chamois begin?	**Wann fängt die Gemsensaison an?**

VOCABULARY

backsight	**die Visierkimme**
barrel	**der Gewehrlauf**
bullets	**die Kugeln**
butt	**der Gewehrkolben**
cartridges	**die Patronen**
ejector	**der Auswerfer**
foresight	**das Korn**
hammer	**der Hammer**
revolver	**der Revolver**
safety catch	**die Sicherung**
telescopic sight	**das Zielfernrohr**
trigger	**der Abzug**

Sailing and Boating

I'd like to hire a dinghy.	**Ich möchte ein Dingi mieten.**
Is an outboard motor extra?	**Kostet ein Aussenbordmotor extra?**

Does this have an auxiliary engine?	**Hat dieser einen Hilfsmotor?**
How many berths are there?	**Wieviele Kojen gibt es?**
How much water does it draw?	**Wieviel Tiefgang hat es?**
Is there a stove/sink/chemical toilet?	**Gibt es einen Kocher/einen Ausguss/eine chemische Toilette?**
Are all cutlery, china and cooking utensils included?	**Is das inklusiv Besteck, Geschirr und Kochgeräte?**
Are sheets and blankets provided?	**Werden Bettlaken und Decken gestellt?**
Have you got a map of the river?	**Haben Sie eine Karte dieses Flusses?**
Are there many locks to negotiate?	**Muss man durch viele Schleusen?**
At what time do the locks close?	**Um wieviel Uhr schliessen die Schleusen?**
How far is it to the next place where I can get fuel?	**Ist es weit bis zur nächsten Stelle, wo ich Kraftstoff bekommen kann?**
Can I leave the boat here while we go to the shops?	**Kann ich das Boot hierlassen, während wir zu den Läden gehen?**
Where is the next refuse dump?	**Wo ist die nächste Abfallgrube?**
Will you please give me a tow?	**Würden Sie mich bitte abschleppen?**

VOCABULARY

anchor	der Anker
boat	das Boot
boathook	der Bootshaken
bow	der Bug
canoe	das Kanu
chart	die Seekarte
deck	das Deck
diesel engine	der Dieselmotor
fender	der Fender
halyard	das Fall
hull	der Rumpf
jib	der Klüver
keel	der Kiel
lifebelt	der Rettungsgürtel
lifejacket	die Schwimmweste
mainsail	das Grossegel
mast	der Mast
motorboat	das Motorboot
oar	das Ruder
paddle	das Paddelruder
pennant	der Wimpel
port (left)	das Backbord
propeller	der Propeller
rowing boat	das Ruderboot
sail	das Segel
sheets	die Laken
starboard (right)	das Steuerbord
to steer	steuern
stern	das Heck
tiller	der Trichter
yacht	die Jacht

Winter Sports

Germany's southern frontier shares with Austria some
beautiful alpine country which provides good skiing territory
of various types. The most famous resort is Garmisch
Partenkirchen where there is an Olympic stadium and the
famous Kandahar downhill race piste. From Garmisch a
railway runs up to Zugspitze, in the Wetterstein range, where
there is snow until the late spring. Another attractive resort
with south-facing slopes is Wank and near the Austrian
frontier is Mittenwald, a village, like its neighbours, of broad-
roofed chalets and painted houses.

I'd like to join the class for beginners/intermediate skiers.	**Ich möchte in die Anfängerklasse/in die Fortgeschrittenenklasse gehen.**
Is there a beginner's slope?	**Gibt es einen Anfängerabhang?**
Where can I hire skis/a toboggan/boots/ski sticks?	**Wo kann ich Schier mieten/ einen Rodelschlitten mieten/ Stiefel mieten/Schistöcke mieten?**
I have never skied before.	**Ich bin noch nie Schi gelaufen.**
These boots are uncomfortable.	**Diese Stiefel sind unbequem.**
They are too tight/loose/big/ small.	**Sie sind zu eng/weit/gross/ klein.**
How far is the ski hoist from the hotel?	**Wie weit ist der Skiaufzug vom Hotel entfernt?**
Can I get a season ticket?	**Kann ich eine Zeitkarte bekommen?**

Are the skiing conditions good this morning?	**Sind die Schneeverhältnisse heute morgen gut?**
Are all the pistes open?	**Sind alle Pisten frei?**
Is there any cross-country skiing?	**Gibt es Schiwanderungen?**
Please help me up.	**Bitte helfen Sie mir auf.**
I think I've twisted my ankle.	**Ich glaube, ich habe meinen Knöchel verstaucht.**
May I join the midnight sledge party?	**Darf ich an der mitternächtlichen Schlittenpartie teilnehmen?**
Two entrance tickets for the ice rink.	**Zwei Karten für die Eisbahn.**
Is there a heated swimming pool?	**Gibt es ein geheiztes Schwimmbad?**
Look out! I can't stop.	**Vorsicht! Ich kann nicht anhalten.**

VOCABULARY

anorak	**der Anorak**
avalanche	**die Lawine**
cable car	**die Seilbahn**
ice	**das Eis**
ice skating	**Schlittschuhlaufen**
funicular	**die Drahtseilbahn**
skates	**die Schlittschuhe**
ski-lift	**der Schilift**
slalom	**der Slalom**
snow	**der Schnee**
stem	**der Stemmbogen**
toboggan run	**die Rodelbahn**

General Services

If you are travelling independently, or have a self-catering holiday at a villa or apartment, phrases for dealing with gas, electricity and plumbing problems will be indispensable. But even when all that is taken care of by someone else, it is useful to be able to communicate with Post Office staff, telephone operators and other officials in their own language.

Post Office

Post Offices in Germany are called **Bundespost** and their mail boxes are yellow, as they are in Switzerland. In Austria letter boxes are blue or yellow. Post Offices are open from 8 a.m., but close for lunch.

Where is the nearest Post Office?	**Wo ist das nächste Postamt?**
What are the opening hours?	**Was sind die Dienstzeiten?**
Can I cash an international money order here?	**Kann ich hier eine internationale Postüberweisung einlösen?**
I want some stamps for a letter to Britain.	**Ich möchte Briefmarken für einen Brief nach England.**
What is the postcard postage rate for the USA?	**Wie teuer ist eine Postkarte nach den Vereinigten Staaten?**
I'd like to register this letter.	**Ich möchte diesen Brief per Einschreiben senden.**
I want to send it by airmail/express/surface/printed matter rate.	**Ich möchte ihn per Luftpost/per Eilboten/normal/als Drucksache senden.**
Where do I post parcels?	**Wo gibt man Pakete auf?**

Do I need a customs form?	**Brauche ich eine Zollerklärung?**
Is there a poste restante here?	**Gibt es hier einen Schalter für postlagernde Sendungen?**
Have you a letter for me?	**Haben Sie Post für mich?**
May I have a telegram form?	**Könnte ich ein Telegrammformular haben?**
I'll send it by the cheap rate/ normal rate.	**Ich möchte es zum billigsten Preis/zum normalen Preis senden.**
When will it arrive?	**Wann kommt es an?**
I want to make a local/an international/a person-to-person telephone call.	**Ich möchte ein Ortsgespräch führen/ein Auslandsgespräch führen/ein Gespräch mit Voranmeldung führen.**
Can I make a reverse-charge call?	**Kann ich ein R-Gespräch führen?**
Switchboard, the line is engaged. Please try again later.	**Fräulein, die Leitung ist besetzt. Versuchen Sie bitte später noch einmal.**

The Police Station

I am a visitor to your country.	**Ich bin ein Besucher Ihres Landes.**
I want to report a theft.	**Ich möchte einen Diebstahl melden.**
a loss.	**einen Verlust melden.**
an accident.	**einen Unfall melden.**

Someone stole my wallet.	**Jemand hat meine Brieftasche gestohlen.**
Something was stolen from my car/my hotel room.	**Etwas ist aus meinem Wagen/Hotelzimmer gestohlen worden.**
The theft occurred in Neuhauser Strasse at about 4 o'clock.	**Der Diebstahl fand ungefähr um vier Uhr in der Neuhauser Strasse statt.**
I have lost my watch on the beach.	**Ich habe meine Uhr am Strand verloren.**
It is valuable.	**Es ist wertvoll.**
It has sentimental value.	**Es hat persönlichen Wert.**
I will offer a reward.	**Ich möchte eine Belohnung aussetzen.**
Someone has been knocked down.	**Jemand ist niedergeschlagen worden.**
A lady has broken her leg.	**Eine Dame hat ihr Bein gebrochen.**
There is a man molesting women on the promenade.	**Ein Mann belästigt Frauen auf der Promenade.**
I have been swindled.	**Ich bin beschwindelt worden.**
Can a police officer come with me?	**Könnte ein Polizist mich begleiten?**
I will be a witness.	**Ich werde als Zeuge auftreten.**
I cannot be a witness. I did not see what was happening.	**Ich kann nicht als Zeuge auftreten. Ich habe den Vorfall nicht gesehen.**

Is there anyone who speaks English?	**Spricht hier jemand Englisch?**

Electricity

The lights have gone out.	**Das Licht ist ausgegangen.**
The power plug is not working.	**Die Steckdose funktioniert nicht.**
The fuse has gone.	**Die Sicherung ist durchgebrannt.**
I think it's the switch.	**Ich glaube es ist der Schalter.**
There is a smell of burning.	**Da ist ein Feuergeruch.**
The stove won't light.	**Der Herd geht nicht an.**
The heating isn't working.	**Die Heizung funktioniert nicht.**
Can you mend it straight away?	**Können Sie es sofort reparieren?**
Where is the fuse box?	**Wo ist der Sicherungskasten?**
Where is the main switch?	**Wo ist der Hauptschalter?**

VOCABULARY

---

adaptor	**der Zwischenstecker**
bulb	**die Glühbirne**
electric cooker	**der Elektroherd**
electric fire	**der elektrische Heizkörper**
extensions lead	**die Verlängerungsschnur**
fuse wire	**der Sicherungsdraht**
hair dryer	**der Haartrockner**

General Services

immersion heater	der Tauchsieder
insulating tape	der Isolierstreifen
iron	das Bügeleisen
plug	der Stecker
radio	das Radio
razor point	die Steckdose für den Rasierapparat
refrigerator	der Kühlschrank
spotlight	die Wandleuchte
television	der Fernsehapparat
torch	die Taschenlampe

Gas

There is a smell of gas.	Hier ist Gasgeruch.
It must be a gas leak.	Das muss ein Gasleck sein.
This is the gas meter.	Dies ist der Gaszähler.
This gas jet won't light.	Diese Gasdüse funktioniert nicht.
The pilot light won't stay on.	Die Zündflamme bleibt nicht an.
Is there any danger of an explosion?	Besteht Explosionsgefahr?
I think the ventilator is blocked.	Ich glaube, der Ventilator ist verstopft.
We can't get any hot water.	Wir bekommen kein heisses Wasser.

Vocabulary

chimney	der Schornstein
gas fire	die Gasheizung

gas light	die Gasbeleuchtung
gas main	das Gashauptrohr
gas pipe	das Gasrohr
gas tap	der Gashahn
geyser	der Badeofen
hammer	der Hammer
key	der Schlüssel
lagging	die Wasserrohrverkleidung
monkey wrench	der Engländer
spanner	der Schraubenschlüssel

Plumbing

Are you the plumber?	Sind Sie der Klempner?
The sink is stopped up.	Der Ausguss ist verstopft.
There is a blockage in the pipe.	Da steckt etwas im Rohr.
The tap is dripping.	Der Wasserhahn leckt.
The tap needs a new washer.	Der Wasserhahn braucht einen neuen Dichtungsring.
This water pipe is leaking.	Dieses Wasserleitungsrohr leckt.
The lavatory cistern won't fill.	Der Spülkasten in der Toilette füllt sich nicht auf.
The valve is stuck.	Das Ventil klemmt.
The float is punctured.	Der Schwimmer hat ein Loch.
The tank is overflowing.	Der Wasserbehälter läuft über.
The water tank has run dry.	Der Wasserbehälter ist leergelaufen.

General Services

basin	das Waschbecken
bath	die Badewanne
cesspool	die Senkgrube
immersion heater	der Tauchsieder
mains water	das Leitungswasser
main drainage	die Kanalisation
overflow pipe	das Überlaufrohr
plug	der Stöpsel
stopcock	der Absperrhahn

Personal Services

This section suggests useful phrases for such occasions as a visit to a doctor, dentist, hairdresser or beautician.

At the Doctor's

Can you recommend a doctor?	**Können Sie mir einen Arzt empfehlen?**
Is there an English-speaking doctor in the resort?	**Gibt es einen englischsprechenden Arzt in diesem Ort?**
Where is the surgery?	**Wo ist die Praxis?**
I have an appointment. My name is ...	**Ich habe einen Termin. Mein Name ist ...**
Can the doctor come to the hotel/house?	**Kann der Arzt ins Hotel/Haus kommen?**
I'm not feeling well.	**Ich fühle mich nicht wohl.**
I feel sick/dizzy.	**Mir ist übel/schwindlig.**
I feel faint/shivery.	**Ich fühle mich schwach/mich fröstelt.**
I have a temperature.	**Ich habe Temperatur.**
a headache.	**Kopfschmerzen.**
back ache.	**Rückenschmerzen.**
a sore throat.	**Halsschmerzen.**
sunburn.	**einen Sonnenbrand.**
diarrhoea.	**Durchfall.**
constipation.	**Verstopfung.**
The pain is here.	**Hier sind die Schmerzen.**
I have been vomiting.	**Ich habe mich übergeben.**
I have hurt my ...	**Ich habe ... verletzt.**

I have been like this since yesterday.	**Mir geht es seit gestern so.**
Do you want me to take my clothes off?	**Soll ich mich ausziehen?**
Is it serious?	**Ist es etwas Ernstes?**
Should I stay in bed?	**Muss ich im Bett bleiben?**
Should I arrange to go home?	**Muss ich zurückfahren?**
I am allergic to ...	**Ich bin gegen ... allergisch.**
I have a heart condition.	**Ich habe ein Herzleiden.**
I am asthmatic/diabetic.	**Ich bin Asthmatiker/ Diabetiker.**
What attention do I get free under the national health arrangements?	**Welche Behandlung ist kostenlos nach den Krankenversicherungs- vereinbarungen?**
Do I have to pay for hospitalization and medicines?	**Muss ich für den Krankenhausaufenthalt und Arzneimittel zahlen?**
It's only a slight problem.	**Es ist nur ein kleines Problem.**

VOCABULARY

PARTS OF THE BODY

ankle	**der Knöchel**
appendix	**der Blinddarm**
arm	**der Arm**
artery	**die Arterie**
back	**der Rücken**
bladder	**die Blase**

blood	das Blut
bone	der Knochen
bowels	der Darm
breast	die Brust
cheek	die Wange
chest	der Brustkasten
chin	das Kinn
collar bone	das Schlüsselbein
ear	das Ohr
elbow	der Ellbogen
eye	das Auge
face	das Gesicht
finger	der Finger
foot	der Fuss
forehead	die Stirn
gland	die Drüse
hand	die Hand
heart	das Herz
heel	die Ferse
hip	die Hüfte
intestine	die Eingeweide
jaw	der Kiefer
joint	das Gelenk
kidney	die Niere
knee	das Knie
leg	das Bein
lip	die Lippe
liver	die Leber
lung	die Lunge
mouth	der Mund
muscle	der Muskel
neck	das Genick
nerve	der Nerv
nose	die Nase
penis	der Penis
rib	die Rippe
shoulder	die Schulter

skin	**die Haut**
spine	**das Rückgrat**
stomach	**der Magen**
tendon	**die Sehne**
testicles	**die Hoden**
thigh	**der Schenkel**
throat	**der Hals**
thumb	**der Daumen**
toe	**die Zehe**
tongue	**die Zunge**
tonsils	**die Mandeln**
urine	**der Urin**
vagina	**die Vagina**
vein	**die Vehne**
womb	**die Gebärmutter**
wrist	**das Handgelenk**

INDISPOSITIONS

abscess	**der Abszess**
asthma	**das Asthma**
blisters	**die Blasen**
boil	**die Beule**
chill	**der Fieberfrost**
cold	**die Erkältung**
convulsions	**der Anfall**
cramp	**der Krampf**
diabetes	**die Zuckerkrankheit**
diarrhoea	**der Durchfall**
dizziness	**das Schwindelgefühl**
haemorrhoids	**die Hämorrhoiden**
hay fever	**der Heuschnupfen**
indigestion	**die Verdauungsstörung**
infection	**die Infektion**
inflammation	**die Entzündung**
influenza	**die Grippe**

nausea	die Übelkeit
rheumatism	der Rheumatismus
shivers	der Schüttelfrost
stiff neck	der steife Nacken
sunstroke	der Sonnenstich
tonsillitis	die Mandelentzündung
ulcer	das Geschwür
whooping cough	der Keuchhusten
wound	die Wunde

At the Dentist's

I need dental treatment as soon as possible.	Ich brauche zahnärztliche Behandlung so bald wie möglich.
I have a toothache/abscess.	Ich habe Zahnschmerzen/ einen Abszess.
My gums are bleeding.	Mein Zahnfleisch blutet.
I have broken my dentures.	Mein Gebiss ist zerbrochen.
Can you suggest a painkiller in the meantime?	Können Sie mir in der Zwischenzeit ein schmerzstillendes Mittel empfehlen?
The bad tooth is at the front/ back/side.	Der kranke Zahn ist vorn/ hinten/an der Seite.
Can you extract it?	Können Sie ihn ziehen?
Does it need filling?	Muss er gefüllt werden?
Can you put a temporary filling in?	Können Sie ihn provisorisch füllen?
Can I bite normally?	Darf ich normal kauen?

Personal Services

I'd prefer gas to an injection.	**Ich nehme lieber Gas als eine Spritze.**
What is your fee?	**Was ist Ihr Honorar?**

At the Optician's

I have broken my glasses.	**Meine Brille ist zerbrochen.**
Can you repair them temporarily?	**Können Sie sie provisorisch reparieren?**
The lens is broken. Can you get a new one quickly?	**Das Glas ist zerbrochen. Können Sie schnell ein neues bekommen?**
Have you got contact lenses?	**Haben Sie Kontaktlinsen?**
I'd like a pair of tinted spectacles.	**Ich möchte getönte Gläser.**
Do you sell binoculars/a magnifying glass/sunglasses?	**Haben Sie einen Feldstecher/ ein Vergrösserungsglas/ Sonnenbrillen?**
I had better have an eye test.	**Ich brauche wohl eine Augenuntersuchung.**
I am shortsighted/long sighted.	**Ich bin kurzsichtig/ weitsichtig.**
How long will it take to make me some new glasses?	**Wie lange dauert es, mir eine neue Brille anzufertigen?**
How much will they cost?	**Wieviel wird sie kosten?**

At the Chiropodist's

I have a painful corn.	**Ich habe ein schmerzhaftes Hühnerauge.**
Can you remove it?	**Können Sie es entfernen?**

My bunion is rubbing against my shoe.	**Mein entzündeter Ballen scheuert gegen meinen Schuh.**
I have a hard spot on the ball of my foot.	**Ich habe eine harte Stelle an meinem Fussballen.**
My nails need attention. One of them is ingrowing.	**Meine Nägel müssen behandelt werden. Einer wächst nach innen.**
Have you anything to soften them?	**Haben Sie ein Mittel, um sie weich zu machen?**
The soles of my feet are very sore.	**Meine Fussohlen sind sehr wund.**

At the Hairdresser's

Where is the nearest hairdresser?	**Wo ist der nächste Friseursalon?**
I'd like to make an appointment.	**Ich möchte mich anmelden.**
I'd like a shampoo and set, please.	**Waschen und legen, bitte.**
I want it cut and shaped, please.	**Schneiden und legen, bitte.**
I wear it brushed forward with a fringe.	**Ich trage es nach vorn gebürstet mit einem Pony.**
I like it brushed back.	**Ich möchte es nach hinten gebürstet haben.**
Can you put some waves/curls in?	**Können Sie es etwas wellen/ Locken legen?**
Brush it back into a bun, please.	**Bürsten Sie es nach hinten in einen Knoten, bitte.**
I would like a colour rinse.	**Ich möchte eine Farbspülung.**

Personal Services

I think I will have it dyed.	**Ich möchte es gefärbt haben.**
Have you a colour chart?	**Haben Sie eine Farbtabelle?**
No hairspray, thank you.	**Kein Haarspray, bitte.**
I'd like a manicure.	**Ich möchte eine Maniküre.**
What is the name of this varnish?	**Wie heisst dieser Lack?**

VOCABULARY

auburn	**kastanienbraun**
blonde	**blond**
brunette	**brünett**
hairdryer	**der Haartrockner**
hairnet	**das Haarnetz**
hairpin	**die Haarnadel**
razor	**das Rasiermesser**
scissors	**die Schere**
to style	**eine neue Frisur machen**

At the Beauty Salon

I'd like a complete beauty treatment, please.	**Ich möchte eine komplette Behandlung, bitte.**
just a facial.	**nur eine Gesichtsbehandlung, bitte.**
to change my make up.	**mein Make-up ändern.**
something more suitable for the seaside.	**etwas Passendes für den Strand.**
something lighter in tone.	**einen helleren Ton, bitte.**

a more open-air look.	**ein natürliches Make-up.**
something for the evening.	**etwas für den Abend.**
I have a delicate skin.	**Ich habe eine empfindliche Haut.**
Can you please suggest a new eye make-up?	**Könnten Sie mir ein neues Augen-Make-up empfehlen?**
I think that is too heavy.	**Ich glaube, das ist zu schwer.**
Have you any false eyelashes?	**Haben Sie künstliche Augenwimpern?**
Perhaps my eyebrows need plucking.	**Vielleicht müssten meine Augenbrauen gezupft werden.**
I'd like to see some new lipstick colours.	**Zeigen Sie mir bitte ein paar neue Lippenstiftfarben.**

At the Laundry/Cleaner's

I'd like them washed and pressed, please.	**Bitte, waschen und bügeln Sie sie.**
Will you iron the shirts?	**Würden Sie bitte die Hemden bügeln?**
I will collect them tomorrow.	**Ich hole sie morgen ab.**
Do you deliver?	**Liefern Sie ins Haus?**
Do you do mending?	**Bessern Sie auch aus?**
This tear needs patching.	**Dieser Riss muss geflickt werden.**
Can you sew this button on?	**Würden Sie diesen Knopf annähen?**

Personal Services

Can you remove this stain? It is coffee/blood/grease/biro.	**Können Sie diesen Fleck entfernen? Es ist Kaffee/ Blut/Fett/Kugelschreiber.**
Can you mend this invisibly?	**Können Sie dies kunststopfen?**
This blouse/coat/dress is not mine.	**Diese Bluse/dieser Mantel/ dieses Kleid gehört mir nicht.**
My trousers are missing.	**Meine Hose fehlt.**
This was not torn when I brought it to you.	**Dies was nicht zerrissen, als ich es herbrachte.**
How long does the launderette stay open?	**Wie lange ist der Waschsalon offen?**

Vocabulary

bleach	**die Bleiche**
clothes hanger	**der Kleiderbügel**
cold/hot/warm water	**kaltes/heisses/warmes Wasser**
launderette	**die Schnellwäscherei**
soap powder	**das Seifenpulver**
washing machine	**die Waschmaschine**

At the Men's Hairdresser

I want a haircut, please.	**Bitte, Haare schneiden.**
Just a trim. I haven't much time.	**Bitte, nur ausputzen. Ich habe nicht viel Zeit.**
Please give me a shampoo.	**Haare waschen, bitte.**
I would like it cut shorter.	**Etwas kürzer, bitte.**

Leave it long, please.	**Lassen Sie es bitte lang.**
You are taking too much off.	**Sie nehmen zu viel weg.**
Take a little more off the back, please.	**Nehmen Sie bitte hinten ein bisschen mehr weg.**
off the sides.	**an den Seiten ein bisschen mehr weg.**
off the top.	**oben ein bisschen mehr weg.**
I part my hair on the left/right.	**Ich trage meinen Scheitel links/rechts.**
I'd like an alcohol rub.	**Ich möchte eine Alkoholbehandlung.**
A singe, please.	**Bitte, sengen Sie die Spitzen.**
Please give me a shave.	**Bitte, rasieren.**
Please trim my beard/moustache/sideboards.	**Bitte, stutzen Sie meinen Bart/Schnurrbart/die Koteletten.**
No thank you, I do not want a facial massage.	**Nein danke, ich möchte keine Gesichtsmassage.**
I will have a manicure.	**Ich möchte eine Nagelpflege.**
May I have a hand towel?	**Könnte ich ein Handtuch haben?**
Put some eau de cologne on but no cream.	**Etwas Kölnischwasser, bitte, aber keine Creme.**
Move the mirror a bit more to the right, please.	**Halten Sie den Spiegel etwas mehr nach rechts, bitte.**
Yes, that's fine.	**Ja, das ist sehr gut.**

153

Making Friends

Good morning/good afternoon/good evening.	**Guten Morgen/guten Tag/guten Abend.**
May I introduce myself?	**Darf ich mich vorstellen?**
May I introduce my friend John/my wife?	**Darf ich meinen Freund John vorstellen/meine Frau vorstellen?**
My name is ...	**Mein Name ist ...**
How do you do?	**Guten Tag.**
Are you staying at this hotel/at this resort?	**Wohnen Sie in diesem Hotel/in diesem Ort?**
Are you enjoying your holiday?	**Verbringen Sie einen schönen Urlaub?**
How long have you been on holiday?	**Wie lange sind Sie schon auf Urlaub?**
Do you always come here?	**Kommen Sie immer hierher?**
I'd like you to meet my friend ...	**Ich möchte Sie mit meinem Freund ... bekanntmachen.**
Would you care to have a drink with us?	**Dürfen wir Sie zu einem Drink einladen?**
What would you like?	**Was möchten Sie?**
Please. I insist that you let me pay.	**Bitte. Dies geht auf meine Rechnung.**
I'm afraid that I don't speak German very well.	**Leider spreche ich nicht sehr gut Deutsch.**
It is very nice to talk to a German person.	**Es ist gut, mit einem Deutschen zu sprechen.**

Which part of Germany do you come from?	**Aus welcher Gegend Deutschlands kommen Sie?**
I am here with my wife/husband/family/friends.	**Ich bin hier mit meiner Frau/meinem Mann/meiner Familie/meinen Freunden.**
Are you alone?	**Sind Sie allein?**
We come from Manchester/England.	**Wir kommen aus Manchester/England.**
Have you been to England?	**Waren Sie schon einmal in England?**
If you come, please let me know.	**Wenn Sie kommen, lassen Sie es mich bitte wissen.**
This is my address.	**Hier ist meine Adresse.**
I hope to see you again soon.	**Ich hoffe, Sie bald wiederzusehen.**
Perhaps you would like to meet for a drink after dinner?	**Vielleicht könnten wir uns nach dem Abendessen zu einem Drink treffen?**
I would be delighted to join you.	**Ich schliesse mich Ihnen gern an.**
When should we meet?	**Wann sollen wir uns treffen?**
Have you got a family?	**Haben Sie Familie?**
Would you like to see some photos of our house and our children?	**Möchten Sie ein paar Fotos von unserem Haus und unseren Kindern sehen?**
Are you going to the gala?	**Gehen Sie zur Galaveranstaltung?**
Would you like to make up a party?	**Möchten Sie sich uns anschliessen?**

Making Friends

It has been so very nice to meet you.	**Es war sehr schön, Sie kennenzulernen.**
You have been very kind.	**Sie waren sehr freundlich.**

Dating Someone

Are you on holiday?	**Sind Sie auf Urlaub?**
Do you live here?	**Wohnen Sie hier?**
Do you like this place?	**Gefällt Ihnen dieser Ort?**
I've just arrived.	**Ich bin gerade angekommen.**
What is there to do?	**Was kann man hier anfangen?**
I don't know anyone here.	**Ich kenne niemanden hier.**
I'm with a group of students.	**Ich bin mit einer Gruppe Studenten hier.**
I'm travelling alone.	**Ich reise allein.**
I'm on my way round Europe.	**Ich bin auf meiner Reise durch Europa.**
I come from Scotland/Australia/ New Zealand/the United States.	**Ich komme aus Schottland/ Australien/Neuseeland/den Vereinigten Staaten.**
Do you mind if I try my German on you?	**Darf ich mein Deutsch an Ihnen ausprobieren?**
My German is not very good.	**Mein Deutsch ist nicht sehr gut.**
Would you like a drink?	**Möchten Sie einen Drink?**
What are you doing this evening?	**Was haben Sie heute abend vor?**

Would you like to go to a discotheque?	**Möchten Sie in eine Diskothek gehen?**
join our party?	** sich uns anschliessen?**
Do you like dancing?	**Tanzen Sie gern?**
Do you like concerts?	**Haben Sie Konzerte gern?**
the opera?	** die Oper gern?**
Can I walk along with you?	**Darf ich Sie begleiten?**
Which way are you going?	**Welchen Weg gehen Sie?**
Do you mind if I sit here?	**Darf ich hier sitzen?**
This is my friend, Tom.	**Dies ist mein Freund Tom.**
Do you have a girl friend?	**Haben Sie eine Freundin?**
We could make a foursome.	**Wir könnten zu viert gehen.**
Do you play tennis/golf?	**Spielen Sie Tennis/Golf?**
Do you go swimming?	**Schwimmen Sie?**
Which beach do you go to?	**An welchen Strand gehen Sie?**
Would you like to come for a drive/a boat ride?	**Möchten Sie eine Autofahrt machen/im Boot fahren?**
It would be nice if you would.	**Es wäre schön, wenn Sie kämen.**
Thanks for coming out with me.	**Vielen Dank, dass Sie mit mir ausgegangen sind.**
I enjoyed it.	**Es hat mir gut gefallen.**
Can we meet again?	**Könnten wir uns wiedersehen?**
How about tomorrow?	**Wäre morgen möglich?**
No, thanks. I'm busy.	**Nein, danke. Ich habe keine Zeit.**

Making Friends

| Please stop bothering me. | Bitte, lassen Sie mich in Ruhe. |

Mutual Interest

Do you play cards/chess?	Spielen Sie Karten/Schach?
Would you like to make a four at bridge?	Würden Sie der vierte Spieler beim Bridge sein?
We play canasta/poker/rummy.	Wir spielen Kanaster/Poker/Romme.
It is an English game.	Es ist ein englisches Spiel.
I'll ask the concierge if the hotel has a chess board.	Ich frage den Portier, ob das Hotel ein Schachbrett hat.
This is your king/queen/knight/bishop/castle/pawn.	Dies ist Ihr König/Ihre Dame/Ihr Springer/Ihr Läufer/Ihr Turm/Ihr Bauer.
We could play draughts or dominoes.	Wir könnten Dame oder Domino spielen.
There is table tennis in the hotel. Would you care for a game?	Es gibt Tischtennis im Hotel. Möchten Sie spielen?
Do you read English?	Lesen Sie Englisch?
Would you like to borrow this book? this newspaper?	Möchten Sie sich dieses Buch leihen? sich diese Zeitung leihen?

Conversations

There are certain universal subjects of conversation which
provide a bridge for communication with strangers all over
the world.

Among these are the weather, families, home, the cost of
living and pets. The following conversational phrases are
designed to start you off on an acquaintanceship with
people who do not speak English. It should, however, be
borne in mind that people do not talk much about the
weather in Germany.

About the Weather

It is a fine day.	**Heute ist ein schöner Tag.**
It's not a very nice day.	**Heute ist es nicht so schön.**
Do you think it will rain all day?	**Glauben Sie, dass es den ganzen Tag regnen wird?**
later?	**dass es später regnen wird?**
tomorrow?	**dass es morgen regnen wird?**
It's going to be hot today.	**Heute wird es heiss werden.**
It's rather windy.	**Es ist ziemlich windig.**
I think there is a thunderstorm coming.	**Ich glaube, wir bekommen Gewitter.**
Look at the lightning.	**Sehen Sie sich die Blitze an.**
It will soon clear up.	**Es wird sich bald aufklären.**
We don't get this kind of weather at home.	**Wir haben solch Wetter nicht bei uns.**
It's a pity it is so dull.	**Schade, dass es so trübe ist.**

Making Friends

Did you see the beautiful sunrise/sunset?	**Haben Sie den herrlichen Sonnenaufgang/ Sonnenuntergang gesehen?**
We had a very good/very poor summer last year.	**Letztes Jahr hatten wir einen sehr schönen/sehr schlechten Sommer.**
There's a lot of haze about today.	**Heute ist es sehr diesig.**
The atmosphere is very clear.	**Die Luft is sehr klar.**
Is it cold here in the winter?	**Ist es hier kalt im Winter?**
I love the spring/summer/ autumn.	**Ich liebe den Frühling/ Sommer/Herbst.**
What does the barometer say?	**Wie steht das Barometer?**

VOCABULARY

breeze	**die Brise**
cloudburst	**der Wolkenbruch**
cloudy	**bewölkt**
drizzle	**der Sprühregen**
dry	**trocken**
forecast	**die Vorhersage**
hail	**der Hagel**
meteorological office	**der Wetterdienst**
mist	**der Nebel**
pressure	**der Druck**
rain	**der Regen**
sleet	**der Graupelregen**
snow	**der Schnee**
sunny	**sonnig**
temperature	**die Temperatur**
weather report	**der Wetterbericht**

About Families

This is my wife/husband/daughter/son.	**Dies ist meine Frau/mein Mann/meine Tochter/mein Sohn.**
My son is an architect/doctor/student/teacher/engineer.	**Mein Sohn ist Architekt/Arzt/Student/Lehrer/Ingenieur.**
My daughter is at school.	**Meine Tochter geht zur Schule.**
She is taking her exams.	**Sie macht ihre Examen.**
Then she will go to university/art school/teacher's training college.	**Dann geht sie auf die Universität/in die Kunstschule/auf die Lehrerausbildungsanstalt.**
She learnt some German at school.	**Sie hat etwas Deutsch in der Schule gelernt.**
My wife is Scottish, but her mother is German.	**Meine Frau ist Schottin, aber ihre Mutter ist Deutsche.**
My father was a teacher.	**Mein Vater war Lehrer.**
The children prefer to have holidays on their own.	**Die Kinder gehen lieber allein auf Urlaub.**
They prefer camping.	**Sie ziehen Camping vor.**
My youngest/eldest son My youngest/eldest daughter is married and lives in ...	**Mein jüngster/ältester Sohn Meine jüngste/älteste Tochter ist verheiratet und wohnt in ...**
Would you like to see some photos of our family?	**Möchten Sie ein paar Aufnahmen von meiner Familie sehen?**

Making Friends

The younger children stayed at home with their grandparents.	**Die jüngeren Kinder sind zu Hause bei ihren Grosseltern geblieben.**
Are these your children?	**Sind dies Ihre Kinder?**
The boy/girl looks like his/her father. his/her mother.	**Der Junge/das Mädchen sieht seinem/ihrem Vater ähnlich. seiner/ihrer Mutter ähnlich.**
How old is he/she?	**Wie alt ist er/sie?**
My daughter is fourteen.	**Meine Tochter ist vierzehn.**

VOCABULARY

aunt	**die Tante**
birthdays	**Geburtstage**
cousin	**der Vetter (male)**
	die Kusine (female)
divorce	**die Scheidung**
father-in-law	**der Schwiegervater**
marriage	**die Ehe**
mother-in-law	**die Schwiegermutter**
relatives	**die Verwandten**
uncle	**der Onkel**
wedding	**die Hochzeit**

About Homes

We have a house in town/in the country.	**Wir haben ein Haus in der Stadt/auf dem Lande.**
It is a detached house with two storeys.	**Es ist ein Einzelhaus mit zwei Stockwerken.**

a semi-detached house.	die Hälfte eines Doppelhauses.
a cottage.	ein kleines Haus.
a maisonette.	eine zweistöckige Wohnung.
a flat.	eine Wohnung.

We have a large garden/a patio.

Wir haben einen grossen Garten/einen Patio.

There are two living rooms. One has a French window and the other a bay window.

Wir haben zwei Wohnräume. Einer hat eine Verandatür und der andere ein Erkerfenster.

There is a fireplace in the dining room.

Es gibt einen Kamin im Esszimmer.

The (whole) house is centrally heated/air-conditioned.

Das (ganze) Haus hat Zentralheizung/Klimaanlage.

We have two garages.

Wir haben zwei Garagen.

The back garden has a lawn, and a swimming pool.

Der Garten hinter dem Haus hat einen Rasen und einen Swimming-Pool.

In our village there are many old houses.

In unserem Dorf gibt es viele alte Häuser.

We prefer a modern house.

Wir ziehen ein modernes Haus vor.

What kind of house have you got?

Was für ein Haus haben Sie?

I like German-style houses.

Ich habe die deutschen Häuser gern.

Do you cook by gas or electricity?

Kochen Sie mit Gas oder elektrisch?

Making Friends

In a warm climate tiled floors are delightful.	**In einem warmen Klima sind gekachelte Fussböden wunderbar.**
Wall-to-wall carpeting makes a house warm in winter.	**Teppichböden machen das Haus im Winter warm.**
Built-in cupboards make a room seem larger.	**Eingebaute Schränke lassen den Raum grösser erscheinen.**
Old furniture is lovely but very expensive.	**Alte Möbel sind herrlich, aber sehr teuer.**

Vocabulary

balcony	**der Balkon**
brick	**der Ziegelstein**
ceiling	**die Decke**
chimney	**der Schornstein**
door	**die Tür**
drains	**die Ableitungen**
foundations	**die Grundmauern**
gable	**der Giebel**
mains electricity	**der Hauptstromanschluss**
gas	**der Hauptgasanschluss**
water	**die Hauptwasserleitung**
plumbing	**die Rohrleitung**
stone	**der Stein**
terrace	**die Terrasse**
tiles	**die Fliesen**
window	**das Fenster**
window frame	**der Fensterrahmen**
window pane	**die Fensterscheibe**
wood	**das Holz**

On Business

I have an appointment with the manager.	**Ich bin beim Manager angemeldet.**
I am from Smith and Company.	**Ich komme von Firma Smith und Co.**
Here is my card.	**Hier ist meine Karte.**
It is good of you to see me.	**Es ist sehr liebenswürdig von Ihnen, mich zu empfangen.**
May I show you our catalogue/samples?	**Darf ich Ihnen unsere Kataloge/Muster zeigen?**
My company manufactures knitwear.	**Meine Firma produziert Strickwaren.**
We are looking for agents.	**Wir suchen Vertreter.**
Our wholesale/retail prices are on this list.	**Unsere Grosshandelspreise/Einzelhandelspreise sind auf dieser Liste.**
There is a special discount for a large quantity.	**Es gibt einen besonderen Mengenrabatt.**
Delivery is within two months/immediate.	**Lieferfrist ist zwei Monate/sofort.**
The prices are f.o.b.	**Die Preise sind f.o.b.**
I would like to see your products.	**Ich möchte Ihre Produkte sehen.**
Have you a showroom in the town?	**Haben Sie einen Ausstellungsraum in der Stadt?**

On Business

What are your terms of business?	**Was sind Ihre Lieferbedingungen?**
Do you already have agents in my country?	**Haben Sie bereits Vertreter in meinem Land?**
Can you make modifications to this model?	**Können Sie dieses Modell umändern?**
May I take some samples with me?	**Darf ich einige Muster mitnehmen?**
I will give you an order now.	**Ich gebe Ihnen jetzt einen Auftrag.**
Can you look after the packing and shipping?	**Können Sie die Verpackung und Verschiffung übernehmen?**
There is only a small market for these goods.	**Der Markt für diese Waren ist nur gering.**

VOCABULARY

balance sheet	**die Bilanz**
banker	**der Bankier**
bill of exchange	**der Wechsel**
certificate	**das Zertifikat**
clerk	**der Angestellte**
contract	**der Vertrag**
correspondence	**die Korrespondenz**
credit	**der Kredit**
debit	**das Debit**
draft	**die Tratte**
export	**der Export**
freight	**die Fracht**
import	**der Import**
insurance	**die Versicherung**
invoice	**die Rechnung**

merchant	der Kaufmann
receipt	die Quittung
remittance	die Überweisung
sale	der Verkauf
warehouse	das Lager

Looking After Your Money

The Bank

Where is the nearest bank?	**Wo ist die nächste Bank?**
Do you accept traveller's cheques at this bank?	**Akzeptieren Sie Reiseschecks in dieser Bank?**
Can I use a Eurocheque card?	**Kann ich eine Euroscheckkarte benutzen?**
Do you issue money against a credit card?	**Geben Sie Bargeld auf eine Kreditkarte?**
I am expecting a remittance.	**Ich erwarte eine Überweisung.**
I have a letter of credit.	**Ich habe einen Kreditbrief.**
I would like a draft to send away.	**Ich möchte eine Tratte schicken.**
What is the rate of exchange for the pound/dollar/Australian dollar?	**Was ist der Umrechnungskurs für das Pfund Sterling/den Dollar/den australischen Dollar?**
What is your commission charge?	**Wie hoch ist Ihre Gebühr?**
I will have it all in 10-mark notes.	**Ich möchte es in zehn Mark-Scheinen haben.**
Please give me 10 marks' worth of change.	**Bitte, geben Sie mir Kleingeld für zehn Mark.**
Can you split this cheque into several currencies?	**Können Sie diesen Scheck in verschiedenen Währungen auszahlen?**

I will have some German marks, Swiss francs and Italian lire.	**Ich möchte D-Mark, Schweizer Franken und italienische Liras.**
Can I open a temporary bank account?	**Kann ich ein provisorisches Konto eröffnen?**
Can you arrange for some money to be sent from my bank in England?	**Können Sie bitte etwas Geld von meiner Bank in England überweisen lassen?**
I seem to be 10 marks short. Can you please count it again?	**Ich glaube, ich habe zehn Mark zu wenig. Könnten Sie es bitte noch einmal zählen?**
Have you a card showing current exchange rates?	**Haben Sie eine Tabelle mit den gültigen Wechselkursen?**

Vocabulary

cashier	**der Kassierer**
cheque book	**das Scheckbuch**
coins	**die Münzen**
credit	**der Kredit**
debit	**das Debet**
deposit slip	**der Einzahlungszettel**
foreign exchange regulations	**die Devisenbestimmungen**
manager	**der Geschäftsführer**
notes	**die Scheine**
signature	**die Unterschrift**
treasury	**das Finanzministerium**

Bureau de Change

Are you open outside banking hours?	**Sind Sie nach den üblichen Dienststunden geöffnet?**

Money Matters

Does the rate of exchange alter outside normal hours?	**Ändert sich der Wechselkurs ausserhalb der Geschäftszeiten?**
Are you open on Sundays?	**Haben Sie sonntags geöffnet?**
Can you show me your rates of exchange?	**Können Sie mir Ihren Wechselkurs zeigen?**
Do you give the same rate for notes as for traveller's cheques?	**Zahlen Sie denselben Kurs für Banknoten wie für Reiseschecks?**

On Losing Traveller's Cheques or Credit Cards

When this happens you should immediately notify the company that has issued the cheques or card but you may need help from a local hotelier or banker.

I have lost my traveller's cheques/credit card.	**Ich habe meine Reiseschecks/ Kreditkarte verloren.**
May I ask them to communicate with me through you?	**Darf ich sie bitten, sich mit mir durch Sie in Verbindung zu setzen?**
Have you a British representative?	**Haben Sie einen britischen Repräsentanten?**
I hope they will be able to replace the cheques quickly. I have no other money.	**Ich hoffe, dass sie die Schecks schnell ersetzen können. Ich habe sonst kein Geld.**
I will ask my bank at home to send some money to you.	**Ich werde meine Bank in England bitten, Ihnen Geld zu überweisen.**
Will you accept a British cheque in payment of the hotel bill?	**Akzeptieren Sie einen britischen Scheck für die Begleichung der Hotelrechnung?**

Reference Section

Numbers

1	eins
2	zwei
3	drei
4	vier
5	fünf
6	sechs
7	sieben
8	acht
9	neun
10	zehn
11	elf
12	zwölf
13	dreizehn
14	vierzehn
15	fünfzehn
16	sechzehn
17	siebzehn
18	achtzehn
19	neunzehn
20	zwanzig
21	einundzwanzig
22	zweiundzwanzig
23	dreiundzwanzig
24	vierundzwanzig
25	fünfundzwanzig
26	sechsundzwanzig
27	siebenundzwanzig
28	achtundzwanzig
29	neunundzwanzig
30	dreissig
31	einunddreissig
32	zweiunddreissig

33	dreiunddreissig
34	vierunddreissig
35	fünfunddreissig
36	sechsunddreissig
37	siebenunddreissig
40	vierzig
50	fünfzig
60	sechzig
70	siebzig
80	achtzig
90	neunzig
100	hundert
101	hundertundeins
110	hundertzehn
200	zweihundert
1000	tausend
1001	tausendundeins
1100	tausendeinhundert
2000	zweitausend
1,000,000	eine Million
1,000,000,000	eine Billion
first	erste
second	zweite
third	dritte
fourth	vierte
fifth	fünfte
sixth	sechste
seventh	siebte
eighth	achte
ninth	neunte
tenth	zehnte
once, twice, three times	einmal, zweimal, dreimal
a half, a quarter, a third, an eighth	ein Halb, ein Viertel, ein Drittel, ein Achtel
a pair	ein Paar
a dozen	ein Dutzend

Time

Greenwich Mean Time	**Westeuropäische Zeit**
Central European Time	**Mitteleuropäische Zeit**
Atlantic Time	**Atlantik Zeit**
Date line	**die Datumsgrenze**
AM/PM	**vormittags/nachmittags**
24-hour clock	**die vierundzwanzig-Stunden-Uhr**
Summertime	**die Sommerzeit**
12.15	**viertel nach zwölf**
12.20	**zwanzig nach zwölf**
12.30	**halb eins**
12.35	**fünf nach halb eins**
12.45	**viertel vor eins**
1.00	**ein Uhr**
midnight/midday	**Mitternacht/zwölf Uhr mittag**

Phrases Referring to Time

What time is it?	**Wie spät ist es?**
It is late.	**Es ist spät.**
It is early.	**Es ist früh.**
Are we on time?	**Sind wir pünktlich?**
At what time shall we meet?	**Wann sollen wir uns treffen?**
At what time are we expected?	**Wann werden wir erwartet?**
On the hour.	**Zur vollen Stunde.**
By the minute.	**Jede Minute.**
Every second.	**Jede Sekunde.**
At regular intervals.	**In regelmässigen Abständen.**
After the clock strikes.	**Nachdem die Uhr geschlagen hat.**

Sunday	**Sonntag**
Monday	**Montag**
Tuesday	**Dienstag**
Wednesday	**Mittwoch**
Thursday	**Donnerstag**
Friday	**Freitag**
Saturday	**Samstag/Sonnabend**
daybreak	**der Tagesanbruch**
dawn	**die Morgendämmerung**
morning	**der Morgen**
afternoon	**der Nachmittag**
evening	**der Abend**
night	**die Nacht**
today	**heute**
yesterday	**gestern**
tomorrow	**morgen**
the day before yesterday	**vorgestern**
two days ago	**vor zwei Tagen**
the day after tomorrow	**übermorgen**
the following day	**am nächsten Tag**
weekday	**der Wochentag**
day off	**ein freier Tag**
birthday	**der Geburtstag**
Christmas Day	**der Weihnachtstag**
New Year's Day	**der Neujahrstag**
All Saint's Day	**Allerheiligen**
May Day (1st May)	**Tag der Arbeit**
weekend	**das Wochenende**
last week	**letzte Woche**
next week	**nächste Woche**
for two weeks	**zwei Wochen lang**
January	**Januar**
February	**Februar**
March	**März**
April	**April**
May	**Mai**
June	**Juni**

July	Juli
August	August
September	September
October	Oktober
November	November
December	Dezember
calendar month	der Kalendermonat
lunar month	der Lunarmonat
monthly	monatlich
since January	seit Januar
last month	letzten Monat
next month	nächsten Monat
the month before	im Monat davor
the first of the month	am Monatsersten
the first of March	am ersten März
BC	v. Chr (vor Christus)
AD	n. Chr (nach Christus)
Leap Year	das Schaltjahr
days	Tage
weeks	Wochen
years	Jahre
day by day	jeden Tag
spring	der Frühling
summer	der Sommer
autumn	der Herbst
winter	der Winter

Temperature Equivalents

FAHRENHEIT		CENTIGRADE
212	Boiling point	100
100		37·8
98·4	Body temperature	37
86		30
77		25
68		20
50		10
32	Freezing point	0
0		− 18

To convert Fahrenheit to Centigrade subtract 32 and divide by 1·8.

To convert Centigrade to Fahrenheit multiply by 1·8 and add 32.

Pressure

The barometer tells you the air pressure of the atmosphere: 15 lb. per sq. in. is normal air pressure at sea level. This equals 1·1 kg. per sq. cm.

A tyre gauge tells you the pressure of your car tyres.

POUNDS PER SQUARE INCH	KILOGRAMS PER SQUARE CENTIMETRES
16	1·12
18	1·27
20	1·41
22	1·55
24	1·69
26	1·83
28	1·97

Measurements of Distance

One kilometre = 1000 metres = 0·62 miles.
One hundred centimetres = 1 metre = 3·3 ft.
One centimetre = 0·39 inches.

The following table gives equivalents for metres and feet.
The figure in the centre column can stand for either feet or
metres and the equivalent should then be read off in the
appropriate column.

METRES	METRES AND FEET	FEET
0.30	1	3·28
0·61	2	6·56
0·91	3	9·84
1·22	4	13·12
1·52	5	16·40
1·83	6	19·68
2·13	7	22·97
2·44	8	26·25
2·74	9	29·53
3·05	10	32·81
3·35	11	36·09
3·66	12	39·37
3·96	13	42·65
4·27	14	45·93
4·57	15	49·21
4·88	16	52·49
5·18	17	55·77
5·49	18	59·05
5·79	19	62·34
6·10	20	65·62
7·62	25	82·02
15·24	50	164·04
22·86	75	264·06
30·48	100	328·08

MILES	MILES AND KILOMETRES	KILOMETRES
0·62	1	1·61
1·24	2	3·22
1·86	3	4·82
2·49	4	6·44
3·11	5	8·05
3·73	6	9·66
4·35	7	11·27
4·97	8	12·88
5·59	9	14·48
6·21	10	16·09
15·53	25	40·23
31·07	50	80·47
46·60	75	120·70
62·14	100	160·93

For motorists it is useful to remember that:

30 miles = 48·3 km.
70 miles = 112·7 km.
70 km. = 43·75 miles
100 km. = 62·50 miles

To convert kilometres to miles, divide by 8 and multiply by 5.

To convert miles to kilometres, divide by 5 and multiply by 8.

Measurements of Quantity

Weight

POUNDS	POUNDS AND KILOGRAMS	KILOGRAMS
2·20	1	0·45
4·40	2	0·90
6·61	3	1·36
8·81	4	1·81
11·02	5	2·27
13·23	6	2·72
15·43	7	3·1752
17·64	8	3·6287

OUNCES	GRAMS
0·5	14·12
1	28·35
2	56·70
3	85·05
4	113·40
5	141·75
6	170·10
7	198·45
8 ($\frac{1}{2}$ lb)	226·80
12	340·19
16 (1lb)	453·59

One kilogram = 1000 grams = 2·2 lb.

Half a kilogram = 500 grams = 1·1 lb.

When shopping for small items, it is convenient to order by the 100 grams; this is about $3\frac{1}{2}$ ounces.

One metric ton = 1000 kilograms.

Liquid Measures

U.K. PINTS	U.K. PINTS AND LITRES	LITRES
1·76	1	0·57
3·52	2 (1 quart)	1·14
5·28	3	1·70
7·04	4	2·27
8·80	5	2·84
10·56	6	3·41
12·32	7	3·98
14·08	8 (1 gallon)	4·55
15·84	9	5·11
17·60	10	5·68

1 litre = 1·76 pints.

One tenth of a litre is a decilitre or ·18 of a pint.

One hundredth of a litre is a centilitre or ·018 of a pint.

One hundred litres are a hectolitre or 22 gallons.

One gallon = 4·6 litres.

One quart = 1·14 litres.

One pint = 0·57 litres.

Clothing Sizes

Measurements for clothes are measured according to the
metric system. Here are the equivalent sizes for the main
articles of clothing:

Women

DRESSES AND COATS

British		34	36	38	40	42	44	46
American		32	34	36	38	40	42	44
Continental		40	42	44	46	48	50	52

Men

SUITS

British and American	36	38	40	42	44	46
Continental	46	48	50	52	54	56

SHIRTS

British and American		14	$14\frac{1}{2}$	15	$15\frac{1}{2}$	16	$16\frac{1}{2}$	17
Continental		36	37	38	39	41	42	43

Index

Index